Books by the author:

WRINKLES: *How to Prevent Them, How to Erase Them*
(with Lida Livingston)

MAKEOVERS

NINE TO FIVE: *A Complete Looks, Clothes and Personality Handbook for the Working Woman*

A Complete Looks, Clothes and Personality Handbook for the Working Woman

CONSTANCE SCHRADER

Prentice-Hall, Inc., Englewood Cliffs, New Jersey

Line illustrations by Glee LoScalzo

*Nine to Five: A Complete Looks, Clothes and
Personality Handbook for the Working Woman,* by Constance Schrader
Copyright © 1981 by Constance Schrader
Address inquiries to Prentice Hall, Inc., Englewood
Cliffs, N. J. 07632
Printed in the United States of America
Prentice-Hall International, Inc., London
Prentice-Hall of Australia, Pty. Ltd., Sydney
Prentice-Hall of Canada, Ltd., Toronto
Prentice-Hall of India Private Ltd., New Delhi
Prentice-Hall of Japan, Inc., Tokyo
Prentice-Hall of Southeast Asia Pte. Ltd., Singapore
Whitehall Books Limited, Wellington, New Zealand

10 9 8 7 6 5 4 3 2 1

Library of Congress Cataloging in Publication Data

Schrader, Constance, date
  Nine to five.

  Bibliography: p.
  Includes index.
  1. Beauty, Personal. 2. Business etiquette.
3. Women—Employment—United States. 4. Women in
business. 5. Work environment—United States.
6. Fashion. I. Title.
HQ1220.U5S35   646.7′042   80-27393
ISBN 0-13-622563-2 (p)
ISBN 0-13-622555-1 (c)

To Ernst-Joseph Schrader, Jr.

Contents

9
5
Getting the Job

The Looks That
Land the Job

This book was written for busy women; people who must get up at the sound of an alarm clock and ready themselves for hours of hectic activity away from the convenience of their own home. They are working people—but as women they want to look their best. On the average, women usually have limited time and limited cash resources. Their crowded schedules may include several hours of work before they leave the house, perhaps an hour traveling time, and between seven and ten hours at work. Then, at the end of the day, they must travel back home, prepare dinner, and tend to homemaking chores. Or, if they are lucky, they return to an active social life where they are expected to sparkle with energy and vitality.

Working women are always on display—they see and are seen by many people every day. Some women see hundreds of people during the day, probably more than their grandmothers saw in months. Sometimes they are seen only fleetingly—perhaps through a car window as they drive by—and sometimes they are scrutinized when they are working closely with a colleague or client, interviewing or being interviewed.

What good is beauty? A great deal of good. Psychologists tell us that the most attractive candidate usually gets the job. Even women bosses prefer attractive women around them. When "beauties" are on the job, they are thought to be more effective and to do their job better than less endowed women. Psychologists are not sure why this is true, but it is. Personnel directors and interviewers for employment agencies all judge candidates by their appearance—whether such a practice is legal or not. This means it is good sense and good business to look your best. The more beautiful you are, the smarter people think you are.

You can be a beauty. Although it requires only a small investment in time and money, some effort is needed because it is one of the job skills that you will have to learn and to master. Like any skill, the effect is cumulative; the more you do, the easier it gets. The little habits of grooming and personal knowledge of what is right for you will soon become second nature and will take very little concentration and planning. The grooming and beauty tips that are included in this book are designed to take as little time as possible. You couldn't possibly use them all. Only a few will be right for you. But keep reading and keep trying.

The book has been divided into four basic units and into eighteen chapters. The chapters are subdivided to provide advice, activities, questions and answers, charts, and tips to save time and money while you become more beautiful. An appendix of reference information is included in the back of the book. Many treatments are suggested that you can use in your spare moments at work, to improve your looks and your potential for advancements.

Beauty is a tool, a gift, and a pleasure. And while it doesn't ensure competence on the job, it can lead to a contentment and happiness that cannot help but ensure an improved performance.

So onward to beauty and success.

Beauty and the Job Interview

There are three dominant elements in your appearance for the job interview: your dress, your makeup and hair styling, and your general demeanor. We will first discuss dress as it is the most immediate thing your potential employer spots when you appear in the waiting room or office doorway for the all-important interview.

Begin by thinking what you would be wearing to work every day if you were employed. If the job calls for a uniform, then it might be best to wear a classic suit to the interview. If you will be working for a glamor firm, such as a music publishing company or a talent agency, you should show a certain flair and originality in your dress, although it shouldn't be too unconventional.

Quite frankly, it often takes guesswork to decide what might be the most appropriate thing to wear, because judgments about you are often made on very personal prejudices.

So when you're in doubt, glance at the outfits charted below. You'll note that the dressing has been broken down to areas of the country—cold, moderate, and warm climates, or cold, moderate, or warm days, depending on the season. The kind of office has also been described as formal or informal. Office work in banks and insurance companies, public relations offices or on newspapers, or in other jobs would be considered formal work situations. Jobs that require a uniform or jobs in factories, outdoors, or in closed areas might be regarded as informal. This is how the most acceptable dress picture looks:

A ZONE CHART FOR JOB-GETTING FASHION

	Work Situation	
	FORMAL	INFORMAL
Warm: Southeast; southern part of the United States; Hawaii	Suit in lightweight fabric or Simple tailored dress	Coordinated jacket and skirt or Blouse and tailored skirt
	Closed shoes, pumps	Sling-back or sandals
	Leather bag	Leather or canvas/fabric bag
Temperate: West coast, central southeast	Suit in light wool	Suit in tweed or corduroy
	Silk blouse or fine cotton shirt or Dress with coordinated jacket	Shirt or blouse Dress with contrasting jacket
	Pumps	Pumps or medium heeled slip-ons
	Light wool coat	Raincoat
	Leather bag	Leather or canvas fabric bag
Cold: Northeast; central midwest; mountain states	Dark or heavy suit	Heavy skirt
	Closed neck blouse or simple sweater	Sweater set
	Closed pumps or fitted boots	Closed shoes or boots
	Heavy full-length wool or leather coat	Car-coat, wool or leather coat
	Leather briefcase or bag	Leather combination tote or bag

And under most circumstances, avoid any man-tailored pantsuits which most dress experts report have an extremely negative effect on personnel directors and employers.

These are the clothing "do's," but there's also a list of clothing "don'ts" for the job interview.

Don't wear anything:

- For the first time
- Stained or spotted
- Needing a hem or missing buttons
- Very different from your own personal style
- Borrowed—and that doesn't really fit

Or:

- An evening or dancing outfit, or anything metallic
- Hose that has a run, or no hose
- Jewelry that clanks or makes noise when you move
- Clothing that includes a designer's name or signature
- Halter necklines
- See-through blouses
- Shorts, bare midriffs
- Slit skirts that open more than two inches above the knee
- Clothing that exposes any underwear

Now let's tackle hair. Your hair is a dominant part of your entire appearance and evokes an immediate reaction in most potential employers.

INTERVIEW HAIRSTYLES

Just as personnel directors react poorly to man-tailored pantsuits on applicants, they respond poorly to very severe or dramatic hairstyles. Short, severe hairstyles have always been associated with military or clerical life for both men and women. Such hairstyles might suggest almost robot-like subservient attitudes and, with them, a rigid personality.

Probably the best hairstyle for a job interview is the style that you usually wear and that you feel most comfortable with. But, of course, it should be modified to be a bit special. The following is just a short list of do's and don'ts that will guide you in your hairstyling:

Do

- Be sure your hair is clean and shining.
- Wear a style that allows full view of your face.
- Wear soft waves or a simple style.
- Wear only simple gold or haircolor (shell) clips, combs, or barrettes in your hair.
- Keep your hair uncovered if at all possible.
- Comb your hair in the ladies' room before the interview.
- Be sure that your hair is freshly colored, if you color it; no dark or light roots showing.

Don't

- Wear dangling hair ornaments; they're distracting.
- Allow your hair to fall across your eyes or face.
- Wear a longer than shoulder-length hairstyle.
- Wear a very curly or frizzy style.
- Wear hair spray or other perfumed hair dressing.
- Wear flowers, bows, or other very elaborate adornments; and don't wear lethal-looking pins or dagger-like pointed ornaments.
- Wear a hat that covers half your face.
- Wear Alice-in-Wonderland long hair or the "spinster's bun" style in variations.

Second in importance to your hair is your makeup. It should show skill in application, attention to details, and expertise in selection and design.

Just as with your clothing, don't try out a new makeup technique or a new color scheme on the day of the interview. You should also consider the lighting that exists in most offices where interviews take place.

As with clothing and your hairstyle, avoid the very severe or very high-styled and daring colors or makeups. But even worse than the latest makeup is the outdated. A recent survey has shown that about 35 percent of the women who experiment with makeup as teenagers wear the same brands and approximately the same color throughout their entire lives.

MAKEUP FOR INTERVIEWS

Let cosmetics make you ageless. They should act not so much as a mask for your maturity, but as an announcement of your experience augmented by your freedom to try the new (but not outrageous). The older a woman is, the more careful and the more alert she must be to changes in makeup color, fashions, and techniques.

The following is a list of makeup do's and don'ts for that all-important interview.

Do's and Don'ts

- Follow your skin tone in your choice of cosmetics.
- Blend several shades to get one even tone that disappears into the skin of your neck.
- Use a water-based makeup for oily areas of your skin; an oil-based makeup for dry areas.
- Never use a foundation that is more than one tone darker or lighter than your natural tone. You cannot make yourself look tanned, only dirty. Tones that are too light make you look sick.
- Don't test makeup on the back of your hand; test it on your neck or the side of your face.
- Don't wear a too-pink foundation. If you need color, or your face is sallow, the color can be provided by blusher.
- Use a tawny blusher with pink overtones. It blends easily with most skins. Use a plum or wine blusher only if your natural color is very dark.
- Make sure your lipstick is neat and your teeth sparkling and clean. When you answer questions, people will be watching your mouth.
- Don't match your eye color to your eyes; use a color that is in the same range as the color you are wearing.
- Rust and earth colors are very popular now, and go well with most complexions.
- Never wear metallic, gilt, or iridescent colors for work.
- Imitate the curve of your eyebrow in applying and blending color.
- Lip color and blusher should be in the same color family.
- Outline your lips with a light brown pencil if you have trouble managing a lip brush.
- Lip gloss makes your lips appear softer and also makes and keeps your lips soft.
- Spray your face lightly with water after your makeup is complete.

- Wear the same makeup that you plan for a job interview for about a week before the interview. Be sure you feel so comfortable in it that you can forget all about it.

The most important thing about dress, hairstyling, and makeup is that they compliment you and create the visual image that will convey your personality, ability, and competence to the interviewer before you even say a word.

PUTTING IT ALL IN ACTION

Now let's approach the question of your general demeanor, which includes posture, handshake, voice, and general body language. Let's first talk about posture. Standing and sitting correctly make you more attractive. Good posture helps avoid cramping your internal organs and it encourages good circulation which will help you think fast and be alert, while chronic bad posture encourages cramping, the shortening of some muscles, and the stretching of others.

Hang a string with a weight on it from the top of a full-length mirror so that the string hangs in a straight vertical line. Then, turning to the side, try to position yourself so that the plumb line passes through the mirror-image of your feet, legs, hips, trunk, shoulders, and head in a vertical line. If you could be seen from the side, when standing, the line should run through your earlobe, touch the tip of your shoulder, pass the middle of the hips, just in back of the kneecap, and pass just in front of the ankle bone.

Now turn and face the mirror: Your feet should be about six inches apart, your head held high as if you were balancing a book. Your chest should be high and out, your stomach and back as flat as possible. Your knees should be slightly flexed, but neither stiff nor locked. Your weight should be distributed evenly with the most weight resting on the balls of your feet.

When walking, your knees and ankles should be limber, your toes pointed straight ahead. Again, keep your chest high and your head high. Swing your legs directly forward from the hip

joints. Your feet should leave the ground—don't shuffle. Come down on the ground with the heel of the foot just a bit before the ball. Swing your shoulders and arms freely. And avoid carrying a shoulder bag or a briefcase always in one arm; that will lead to overworking one side of your body.

The position of your hips is often the key to your posture. Your hips should rest squarely upon your legs without tilting either forward or backward.

A potbelly or a thick waist is frequently due to poor posture If your abdominal muscles are weak, your stomach tends to sag and your internal organs slump forward. The result: a protruding stomach, a curved lower back—and backaches.

High-heeled shoes can throw off your center of gravity. Also, the muscles of the calves and back of the thighs become shortened. However, this need not occur if you change your shoes often and occasionally wear low-heeled shoes.

"Chicken neck," a position in which the head is poked forward and is out of line with the shoulders, is another common posture fault.

Learn to sit gracefully, since you will be spending most of your time during the interview sitting down.

Sit tall and far back in the chair; don't perch on the edge. Keep your feet flat on the floor. Keep your chest up and out. The back of your neck should be nearly in line with your upper back. When you are leaning forward, or writing, lean forward from the hips so that you keep your head in line with your shoulders.

Get the "feel" of proper posture positions. Practice makes perfect—perfectly poised and graceful.

The handshake that begins the interview will tell both you and the interviewer a lot about each other. A professor at Tulane University recently noted that a handshake can reveal personality. If your interviewer shakes hands:

- With the arm extended and with the hand at arm's length, he or she is pleasant and easy to work with, and will meet you more than half way.
- With hesitation in extending the hand, even after you have extended yours, he or she is cautious in committing to an idea.
- With eyes lowered, watching the hand rather than looking at your face, he or she might be shy, or someone who is sensitive and diplomatic.

- By pumping your hand in an up-and-down motion, he or she has a dominant personality; by swinging your hand from side to side, he or she is a relaxed, very friendly, and outgoing person.
- And wipes his or her hands either before or after shaking, this action is suspect; it might mean a real dislike of contact with people.

A handshake can indicate a greeting, but it can also be a form of monitoring or control. Be wary of people who hold your hand too long or seem reluctant to release it.

Once the job interview has started, don't hesitate to ask to open a window if you feel nervous or hot. The interviewer will probably want to make you feel relaxed and comfortable. If he or she doesn't or if the person seems to enjoy your natural anxiety, that will tell you something about the kind of people you will be working with and the company. Keep in mind:

- The skills or tasks that will be required; get as specific an answer as possible
- The reporting relationships, who will be making major decisions and who reports to whom
- The personality styles of the people in the company
- The specific medical, vacation, and time requirements and benefits provided by the company
- The future opportunities that might develop from proficiency displayed on the job
- The number or kind of people with whom you will work closely

Don't hesitate to ask if anyone has ever failed at the job you are applying for, and the reason for the failure. The answer that you get to this question might be the most important one of the interview. (If you are interviewing for a job as an administrative aide, it might be interesting to know that the last person lost the job because she didn't like to work evenings.)

If the interviewer has a copy of your resume, you might want to go over points and amplify them, or explain what might seem an odd bit of information, such as a missing year or two.

The interviewer will want to make you feel relaxed and will enjoy a pleasant conversation with you, and want to "draw you out." The idea is to evaluate the type of person you are and find any related usable experiences and skills that you might have that might help on the job. It is as important for the employer as for you to be sure that your needs, interests, goals, and skills are the same. More job problems are caused by miscommunication than by incompetence.

Whether or not there is any formal evaluation of you and your skills, you will probably be evaluated on many of the following points:

- Sincerity, and pleasant manner
- Conversational style
- Ability to listen, respond, and answer in an organized manner
- Attitude toward work and people
- Emotional maturity
- Capacity for hard work and your interest in the work
- Initiative, sense of humor, values, sense of responsibility, drive, determination, and leadership potential
- Status needs and long-term goals

In talking to the interviewer, be very aware of the kinds of questions that are asked. It is illegal to be asked:

- Your religion
- Your parents' origin of birth or citizenship
- Marriage plans, or living situation
- Training or experience other than what might be logical for the job (for example, if you are a nurse, you cannot be expected to know shorthand)

You cannot be refused a job on the basis of age, sex, a physical handicap, or a term in jail. Leading questions about these subjects are just as illegal as direct questions.

Once you're sure that you have looked your best and have represented yourself most honestly, the next step is ending the interview. Most interviews last about half an hour, some are as long as an hour and a half, but they usually don't last longer than that. Be aware of the interviewers' body signals and the finality in their tone as cues to when the interview is over. Usually they will make some announcement or summing up. Or they will rise and walk toward the door, or announce how long it might take before any reaction to the candidate's interview can be expected.

The last thing to say is a simple "Good-bye." Leave as soon as possible, but take note of the people who are working, what they wear, how well-groomed they are, what sort of lighting and ventilation is provided, and if the office seems pleasant. If you have decided against the job before you leave, say so. But if you are interested in the job, later write a letter reassuring the employer, and providing any additional information you might have, or might have been requested to supply.

Now reward yourself. Buy flowers, a pretty scarf, a best-selling book, or a record.

REVIEWING THE INTERVIEW

After a few hours, or that evening, think back on the interview. List the points you made that are important, and the responses that went well. You should also review your makeup, hairstyle, and the garment you selected to wear for the interview. Did you feel completely comfortable? Did you feel relaxed and were you really unaware of yourself and able to concentrate on the questions during the interview?

Whether or not you get the job, all the effort involved in beauty preparation is never lost. The nice thing about practice and perfection in grooming techniques is that you keep adding to your skills. Everything you learn can be used every day, all day, so that you can look your best easily and quickly.

Fashion in the Work World

Now we're going beyond the clothes that land the job and are ready to consider what you may need for your everyday professional life.

Being well-dressed affects people who wear uniforms as well as those who must take something different from their closets every day.

While fashions change, and the details change, the continuing measure for selection should be what makes you look healthy, youthful, vital, intelligent, and suitable. You may have other goals, too—clothes can make you look serious, elegant, authoritative, soft, gentle, womanly, even sexy.

Moreover, your clothes should be appropriate, clean, well-fitted, and flattering. They should require a minimum of care, and in addition they should be of a color and texture that is especially suited to your figure and complexion.

All of this is possible. The following is a group of ideas, rules, guides, and suggestions. Take the ones that work for you. (Remember, nothing works for everyone. So modify any of the following to suit your own unique characteristics.)

COLOR CAN WORK FOR YOU

Let's start with color, a number one consideration in planning your wardrobe. Sometimes the psychological impact of color on people can be profound. People, it has been shown, react more to color than to cut.

Red, for example, is a great color for bolstering your spirits and those of the people around you. If red seems too dramatic, try wine or pink. A uniform wearer can even choose pink.

Yellow and orange mean energy, intellect, and imagination. But, avoid orange if you are interested in management, banking, or any conservative profession. And confine yellow or orange to blouses and sweaters, whatever your job.

Green in metallic shades should be avoided; rather, stick to khaki and avocado. Light greens have a tendency to look unflattering under certain kinds of light. If you're a brunette, dark green can be very flattering.

Blue is a good-taste color. An entire wardrobe can be built around it. Ideally, light and dark shades of blue complement each other.

Brown, combined with black, very deep blue, or beige, can look expensive. However, it isn't an inviting color and should not be worn too often. Brown is a "service" color and people will expect service from you if you wear it too often.

Camel, beige, cream, and white are all wonderful any time, any place, and any climate. If you cannot be a blonde, you can achieve the softness of being a blonde by wearing these champagne to wheat shades.

Black and gray are both traditional and dramatic colors that look well on most people.

Avoid off shades: lavenders and indigos. But steer toward peach; deep purple; wine; warm, glowing brown; and umbers. When you select a color, be sure that it is one that might appear in nature. Don't wear unnatural colors. They are shocking and disconcerting. And if you are over fifty, generally it's wise to avoid electric blue, shocking pink, orange, pea green, aqua blue-green, and greenish browns.

Last of all on the subject of color—if your boss has a favorite color, wear it.

FABRIC IS IMPORTANT
FOR THE RIGHT IMPRESSION

Fabric is next in importance in clothing selection. People react more to it than to the garment's silhouette. To look as elegant as possible, you should choose natural fibers. They are comfortable in all temperatures, wear well, return to their shape immediately, and can be washed in cold water. The difference between polyester, acetate, acrylic, nylon, or other man-made fibers and the natural fibers such as cotton, linen, and wool is the difference between leather shoes and plastic ones: comfort, fit, wear, durability, and beauty.

But, if you really find yourself more comfortable in synthetic fabrics, select the ones that are in a color and texture most like that of a natural fiber. And always select fabrics that are non-reflective, smooth, even in texture and color.

The naturals:

Cotton is one of the few fabrics which translates well into prints—hand-painted or silk-screened fabrics, African and South Pacific cottons. Plaid, striped, or other patterns where the color is woven directly into the fabric, as well as Liberty of London and provincial prints of southern France are also acceptable for office wear.

Linen has a strong natural texture and should never be printed. The most elegant linen dresses are of a solid color, and very simply cut. Rayon can in a small way duplicate the best properties of linen, but it soon loses shape. Many people feel that linen is impractical because it creases so easily. But there is nothing as attractive, sexy, and luxurious as creased white linen in a simple tailored suit.

Silk is the most attractive of all fibers because it is warm, light, durable, flexible, and takes color so well. A silk wardrobe is the height of luxury. Tailored clothes in silk are perfect for any office/work situation. But here are two things to keep in mind about silk. It is fragile and stains easily. And when you select it in prints, you should choose only classic designs such as paisley or stripes.

Wool is the most versatile of fabrics. It springs back to shape quickly and needs little pressing. It can be worn in varying weights in any climate. It can be woven into a large variety of finished fabrics, and of course, knitted, knotted, and dyed in many different colors. Because wool can be treated in so many different ways, printed wool is not as popular for prints as cotton or man-made fibers. Tweeds, twills, and plaids are popular wool patterns. But, beware: No more than one distinct texture should be worn at any one time. Although fashion magazines tout pattern-on-pattern, even very few models can wear it well.

Fabrics that are usually flattering include:

- Crepe silks
- Cottons, closely woven
- Linens
- Wools, challis, and lightweight fabrics
- Flannels and felts
- Flat, close-knitted fabrics
- Velvet
- Corduroy

Fabrics that may be unflattering or unsuitable for the office include:

- Rough tweeds
- Plaids or twill fabrics
- Bulky mohair or fuzzy fabrics
- Shiny fabrics, such as satin
- Stiff silks that have a strong sheen (often seen in Oriental silks, especially Indian and Chinese fabrics)

CARE IN CUT AND STYLE

After color and fabric, you'll need to consider the right silhouette to wear for your particular figure.

If you are *heavy:* Wear V-necks and low oval necks; and dress in one color, or a blend of one color. Keep your clothes simple. Don't wear heavy fabrics, or printed or plaid jackets. Avoid all large prints, wide-fitted bodices, tight belts, dirndl skirts, and turtleneck sweaters. Wear tent dresses, with dark or contrasting lines running the length of the garment. When you wear a scarf, tie it loosely. Wear full-length coats rather than short jackets. Avoid any garments with pocket trimmings of a contrasting color.

If you are *heavy but tall:* Wear set-in sleeves, carefully tailored clothing of flat, woven fabrics. Avoid knitted fabrics, shirt-style blouses, tunic overblouses, capes, dolman sleeves, overblown draperies. If you are heavy but long-waisted, you can wear ribbed sweaters and long sleeves that add grace to your arm movements.

Thick-waisted: If you carry any weight on your stomach or middle, wear garments without waistlines, coat dresses, long vests, or jacket-shirts.

Wide-hipped: If your hips are wide, keep any bright color on the upper part of your body.

Tall and thin: It is a fallacy that the tall and thin can wear anything. If clothes are too tight, you can look scrawny. If they are too loose, you can look like a stick inside of a sack. When your neck is corded and wrinkled, avoid "jeweled" necklines. Choose high, soft, or Byronesque collars, scarves, and soft bows. Avoid décolletés. (They are great for Elizabeth Taylor, but thin Jackie Onassis no longer wears them.)

Keep the arms covered with lightweight fabrics and sleeves. Do not wear sleeveless dresses, tops, or shirts, and if you do wear short sleeves be sure the edge of the sleeve is well-fitted against the arm. Avoid baggy or loose clothing. Keep all clothes close to the body. Gathered or pleated skirts would be most attractive on you, but be sure that the waist fits correctly and that all the clothing is neat and close-fitting. Tight vests will flatter.

Short and thin: Dress with dignity. Beware of looking like a tiny imp. Everything should be selected for proportion and fit. If you have passed thirty, do not buy your dresses in the children's shop—even though you might have been able to do that in earlier adult life. However, you still might find pea jackets and small-sized slightly tailored shirts that can be worn for sportswear in a preteen shop. Be sure your clothing fits correctly, and allow yourself the joy of very bright colors, and bright, dashing scarves.

Here is a list of specific problems and some specific solutions:

Neck—scrawny, corded, sagging, wrinkled: Use pastel and bright-colored scarves in soft light fabrics and attractive subtle patterns or textures. Wear high-necked tailored shirts, collars of pearls, beads, or softly woven fabrics. Keep away from anything worn tightly around the neck, instead stick to soft cowls, turtlenecks, and hoods.

Shoulders—scrawny, bony, winged back: Use soft shawls and scarves. Make ponchos out of soft summer fabrics to wear over open dresses. Use soft shoulder pads in suits and blouses and jackets. (No Joan Crawford "thirties" look!) Be very careful that the back of the neck of all garments fits correctly. So often the backs of jackets or dresses that close with a zipper pouch out on thin people.

Breasts—small or poorly shaped: Avoid sleeveless dresses, halters, strapless dresses, or low-cut armholes. Wear set-in sleeves, and select blouses and tops that are carefully darted in the bodice.

Breasts—too large: Loose enough through the chest, but neat at the shoulders; no muu-muu type garments. All clothes must be fitted.

Abdomen and waist—soft and sagging: Wear skirts and sweaters or blouses of the same color, avoid belts. Be sure that the waists are big enough so the flesh does not lop over the waistband. Avoid anything with pockets on or near the waist. Wear tunics, overblouses, wide sleeves, tent dresses in firm but not stiff fabrics. Do not wear jersey blouses or knits.

Upper arms—sagging skin, folded armpits, wrinkled elbows, heavy upper arm, hanging flesh: Never wear binding sleeves, open sleeveless dresses or blouses. Wear loose sleeves. Select styles that are full in the arm, but carefully fitted at the shoulder.

Lower arms—veined, stringy or scrawny: Choose long-sleeved blouses and dresses. In the summer, stick to thin cotton shirts. Don't wear large or eye-catching bracelets. Avoid very large, massive, or masculine watches.

Elbows—tough, scaling, saggy skin: Wear over-the-elbow sleeves. To improve the state of your elbows, don't rest them on tables and cream them nightly.

Buttocks—large, soft, flat, sagging: Tight slacks are worse than tight skirts. Avoid double-knit fabrics. Stick to woven, firm fabrics; do not ever wear knitted skirts. When wearing slacks, be sure the seat area fits closely and is more than two inches larger than you are. Remember, you expand when seated. You will look slimmer. (The average buttock spread is eight to ten inches when sitting.) And don't forget, it's never too soon to start exercising to tone up this part of your body.

Belly—protruding, sagging, tired: If the area below the waist folds in any way when seated, you have a problem. Avoid knitted fabrics. Wear jackets open; wear your skirts with the waist carefully fitted so that the belly protrudes as little as possible.

Avoid pleats, double-thickness fabrics, pockets, belts, dirndls, and any other style that draws attention to the lower body. Front-closing styles such as the shirtwaist are good. The distended belly can also be hidden by tunics, long vests, jacket-shirts, soft flowing fabrics, and styles that fall directly from the bust to the upper thigh.

Thighs—thick, soft, with the "sandbag look," or bony with knobby knees: No tight slacks but, at the same time, avoid voluminous ballooning coverings. Call attention to the waist, upper part of the body, and feet. Long jackets, and the same tricks that disguise the large buttocks or flat buttocks, can be used.

LOOKING BEST FOR LESS

Clothes protect us, keep us warm, and account for a good percentage of every working woman's yearly expenses. A recent American management research division report stated that the average working woman spends almost $1,700 a year on clothes and grooming aids for her job. According to a nationwide study, the major expenditures are:

Pantsuits	$277	Jackets (blazers)	$151
Dresses	$275	Pants (slacks)	$139
Skirt suits	$243	Skirts (dresses)	$121
Shoes	$199	Sweaters and blouses	$280

You'll notice that most of the expense is above the waist, and that skirts are a small item in comparison to pants and pantsuits. However, the current trend is away from pants and back toward skirts. With the return of skirts, more and more focus on shoes will be seen.

Note that this survey doesn't take into consideration the money that is spent on underwear: A good slip can cost about $15, and bras and pantyhose are more and more expensive each passing day.

It is impossible to recommend a basic wardrobe without knowing what your lifestyle is like. But the list below will give you an idea. It is divided regionally—north, central, and south—and into expensive and less expensive wardrobes.

EXPENSIVE	LESS EXPENSIVE
North	
Navy blue suit, gray flannel suit	Corduroy suit
Two silk blouses, white and a dark basic color	White silk blouse
Lined raincoat suitable for wear from fall through winter (Burberry's $300 coat is worth it)	Yellow slicker raincoat
	Quilted winter coat
Tweed or brown skirt	Corduroy Skirt
White cashmere sweater	Wool sweater
Pumps in black or brown	Pumps in black or brown
Boots	Boots
Leather briefcase or attache case or bag	Canvas or leather tote or bag
Central	
Two flannel or tweed suits	One suit, tweed; one knitted suit or matching sweater and skirt
Slicker, rubber or unlined raincoat	Beige cloth raincoat
Three blouses; three shirts	A blouse and a shirt
Silk jersey dress	Two lightweight wool dresses
Pumps	Pumps
South	
Beige linen suit	Cord suit or light blue or beige cotton suit
White linen skirt	Beige Skirt
White flannel skirt	
Navy blue jacket in linen or very light wool	Two cotton blouses, long sleeves
Three cotton blouses with short sleeves	Two cotton t-shirts, short sleeves
	One t-shirt dress
One pair sling-back leather pumps	One pair sling-back fabric pumps
One pair leather sandals	One pair cloth sandals
Leather case in light beige	Straw case or bag

A word about lingerie:

Pantyhose: Keep at least six pairs on hand in your home and two pair in your office drawer at all times. They must fit exactly and be the right shade. Use a slightly lighter shade if you have thin legs, and a darker shade if you have heavy legs. Avoid pantyhose with seams, clocks, or embroidery on them. They are suitable for chorus lines, and disco dancing, but not for office wear. Once you have found a color you like and a style that fits, don't settle for substitutes. If need be, write the manufacturer and find out where you can get the hose. You might also offer to buy it directly. If the price is right, it might be sensible to get a dozen pairs and save money and time.

With open-toed shoes, wear sandalfoot hose. There is never any excuse for anything else. Never.

Panties: If you have to wear panties with your pantyhose, you should see your gynecologist. There is no reason to suffer even the mildest discharge. If modesty makes you wear panties, cotton wears best and is best ventilated to avoid vaginal discharge problems. Buy them with flat edges around the leg so they don't bump or bulge under your clothing. The most chic French and Italian women buy American underwear because it is the best in the world. European underwear looks fine when new, but ours wears the longest and is the most comfortable.

Bras: If you are over size 32A or over age thirty, wear a bra at all times, except when sleeping. The breasts should spread naturally when you are lying flat, but the constant weight of a breast when you are in an erect position subjects the tissue to gravity pull: years of that sags chins and breasts.

Slips and petticoats: Your undergarments should protect your clothes, not confine your movements. Be sure that the elastics do not bind around the waist. It is better to have loose comfortable slips than to have to replace your underwear after just a few wearings because the seams are tearing.

As soon as your underwear looks the least bit worn, discard it. It is a small luxury to have immaculate and crisp underwear. It is actually an investment when you consider how much better your clothes will wear with underwear that protects your clothes.

ACCESSORIES

Accessories should be kept to a minimum. The fewer things that are carried, and the less "busy looking" you appear, the better.

Accessories include gloves, hats, shoes, handbags, and pantyhose, all the articles of clothing that are not included in the basic ensemble. They also include jewelry, bracelets, earrings, necklaces, pins, brooches, pendants, watches, scarves, belts, umbrellas.

It's practical and money-saving to keep your wardrobe of leather accessories to one color that goes with most of your clothing: black, brown, wine, navy blue, or gray. A basic set of winter accessories and summer accessories of the best possible quality is a very good investment.

For your gloves, you'll want:

- Wrist-length, unlined
- Wrist-length, silk-lined
- Wrist-length, fur- or cashmere-lined.

Then you'll need a handbag in leather or canvas for daily office wear and sportswear.

Or, you can carry a small bag of leather or fabric inside your briefcase, if you prefer it to a large handbag. A classic briefcase looks smart and effective, and it can double for an overnight case. No matter what you carry in it, you always look neat and proper. A leather briefcase is not really a luxury. Keep checking men's departments and luggage stores until you find the right case on sale.

Whether you select a case or bag, be sure that the one you get is free of any brass, metal, chain, or other ornament. It should be as simple as possible in an envelope, pouch, or box shape, the straps attached so that they hold the entire weight of the bag or case. And avoid any case with initials, or one that's a canvas and leather combination. Suede does not wear as well as leather.

Tote bags are used for almost everything. In the winter, many people wear boots and carry along an extra pair of shoes for indoor wear; in the summer a bag is often used for swimming gear, or for a shawl or sweater that can be taken out in air-conditioned rooms and restaurants. Select a bag that will blend with or exactly match your leather handbag. Leather is always best, but cloth bags are convenient because they can be folded when not in use. Again, avoid busy, bright, and very ornate designs. And, most of all, avoid quaint sayings and announcements of all kinds.

Shoes and Boots: These are among your most important accessories. A clumsy pair of shoes, or messy misshapen shoes, can do more to hurt your work image than anything except smeared lipstick.

If you work in an office, wear classic expensive-looking pumps in either black, wine, or brown with the latest style heels, as high as you can tolerate. Keep them at your desk if they're too uncomfortable to wear to and from work. Remember: To look feminine is in your favor. Of course, if you're on your feet all the time, you'll need shoes that are very comfortable, and hang the appeal.

The rule for boots is the same as for shoes. Keep them as sensual, simple, and expensive as possible. Shoes and boots are often fetish objects for men, and even the most "normal" (if there is such a thing as a normal person) are fascinated by feet and shoes and will often notice a woman's shoes.

The rule for boots is never to show any leg between the top of the boot and the bottom of your skirt. Your skirt should always be long enough to cover the boot top. Ankle-length boots should be reserved for informal wear, and then worn only with slacks.

Hats: Use a beret or simple wool cap for the coldest weather. On other days, a small brim hat in felt is businesslike. Keep a kerchief of wool, silk, or cotton in your bag or briefcase for all sorts of emergencies. But always avoid plastic hats. They're tacky and bad for your scalp.

Belts: Belts are one of the accessories that most people should avoid. If your waist is less than 24 inches, you can wear any sort of belt you want. If it is between 24 and 30 inches, wear only the finest leather of a color that exactly matches the fabric of the garment you are wearing. If you are larger than 30 inches, never wear an "accessory" belt, and study well any dress that includes a self-belt. Even the same color and fabric tends to "cut the line." And it may be more flattering to find a style without a belt.

If you have a belted coat or some of your garments have belts, and your waist is more than 30 inches, see if the belts can be removed. If not, wear the belt or tie sash loosely, calling as little attention to it as possible.

The only belt buckle that is attractive is a small gold or silver buckle, round or square in shape. The only exception to this is a Western belt.

Umbrellas: Umbrellas are great for keeping the rain and the sun away, but only if they are large enough. If they are not adequate in diameter, they are silly looking and they leave you with wet shoes and ankles. If you are over five feet four inches tall, use a man's black silk umbrella, one that is light in style, has strong wire ribs, and a simple handle. Use a folding one if you can manage it, as all umbrellas are clumsy to carry.

If you are less than five feet four inches, or want to use a woman's umbrella, avoid a fussy or frilly model, or one that is printed with any design. Select a basic color; one the same as your handbag is best. Look for a handle that is the same color as the fabric covering. Do not use an umbrella that has fake jewels or anything shiny on the handle, and avoid ribbon or chain handles.

Never use printed paper shopping bags—but do keep one with you for an emergency. And never, never use two thicknesses of paper shopping bag. This really gives a "bag lady" appearance.

Jewelry: The most popular piece of jewelry is a watch. Worn by singles and marrieds, of all ages and both sexes, selling from $5.95 to $5,000, watches are designed to do one thing: Tell time. It is very difficult to find the right watch for almost every occasion or costume, but as a basic rule watches should never attempt to be anything other than what they are. A watch is not a bracelet.

The best watches are plain, man-styled—gold watches that are square or round in shape. They can be attached to black suede, leather, patent leather, or self-bands.

An antique watch, pinned to your jacket or shirt with a small Victorian gold pin, or even a plain gold safety-style pin, is preferable to a plastic-faced watch, which would better fit a Little League baseball player.

Since a watch is probably a piece of jewelry that you wear every day and that you look at several times during the day, buy the best for your budget. Invest in the case, the style, and the workings of the mechanism. It should be real gold.

Roman numerals are as popular as Arabic numerals, and

presently no-numeral faces of a flat color are in vogue. Avoid color watches, unless you select white or black, and until computer-digital watches become available in gold cases with reliable guarantees for more than a year, don't invest in one.

Necklaces: A single strand of pearls is best. They should be of a creamy, even pinkish, color, and well-matched. They can be cultured or frankly fake, but the clasp should be attractive and the pearls should be expensive-looking, since they are so plainly in view. The size of the pearl is up to the wearer, and the length is also a subject of personal preference. In general, tiny pearls look foolish on a large woman; and a tiny woman should avoid large beads. Graduated pearl necklaces have a dated look; select a necklace that has matched pearls of the same size.

Recently, pearls have been replaced by gold chains in fashion. Pearls or chains can be worn at almost any time with almost any outfit.

If you have diamonds, wear them. Wear them every day with suits or uniforms. Dinah Shore was one of the first to introduce diamonds with a casual day dress—a plain, short chain of diamonds worn with a sleeveless, scoop-necked white pique. The look was great when she introduced it, and it's great today. Don't wear emeralds, rubies, garnets, or colored stones unless in a solitaire ring. It is best to avoid wearing more than one colored stone. Although diamonds make a good marriage with emeralds, multicolored jewelry should be avoided.

Semiprecious stones can be effective, but they are generally better for leisure wear.

Don't ever wear imitation jewelry unless it is forthrightly that—imitation. While fantasy gems can be delightful for informal or holiday wear, garish costume jewelry can make a very tacky impression.

Jewelry shouldn't make noise when you move. Clanging bangles or chains, and other moving jewelry, are cheap attention-getters. Don't wear charm bracelets, whether or not they announce the age and number of relatives, birth signs, or your hobbies. They are very out of fashion.

School and club rings are also better avoided. There is nothing more pathetic than a high school or college graduation ring worn on a hand that is spotted with age.

Wedding and engagement rings should be selected for sentimental reasons, and worn for those reasons rather than for fashion.

Wear a favorite small pin that is a family keepsake or the same simple pin or clip every day if it is your "signature." But don't load yourself down with bangles.

Audrey Hepburn has retained her image as a beauty without any jewelry; and even such a sex goddess as Marilyn Monroe was very careful not to overload herself or detract from her personal image in any way. Think of yourself as the most basic and most precious ornament, and care for your skin, hair, and nails endlessly rather than invest time or money in a passing trinket.

A last word about fashion:

Less is more, as the famous architect Mies van der Rohe said. After you are all dressed, count up the basic parts that make up your outfit. Remember that each piece of jewelry counts as one point, a patterned outfit counts as an extra point, a belt that is bright and noticeable counts as a point, a pair of textured panty-hose is a point by itself.

If you can keep yourself within seven points, you're probably well-dressed. If you have more than ten points, take something off. Chic is simple!

9
5
On the
Job

On-the-Job Skin

Even if you work in drying air conditioning or out-of-doors, you can have smooth, glossy, tautly elastic and blemish-free skin at all times. With the newer makeups, you can actually give your skin a beauty treatment at the same time you are looking pretty and groomed. The correct cosmetic treatment comes with selecting the cosmetic care that is right for your skin texture, color, and acid/alkali balance. To learn about your special skin, look at the questions below and answer *yes* or *no* to each of them.

General Health

- Do you often seem flushed?
- Are there any broken veins on your skin?
- Do you have many freckles or spots on your skin?
- Do you bruise easily?
- Is your skin often blotchy or sensitive?
- Are you allergic to any skin preparations?
- Does your skin ever feel itchy and uncomfortable?

Contour and Tone

- Do you have any loose or sagging skin?
- Do you have any deep wrinkles?
- Do you have crepey skin?
- Do you have bags or fatty deposits under your eyes?

Oiliness

- Do you have enlarged pores on your nose or chin?
- Do you have a tendency to blackheads or whiteheads?
- Do you often have pimples?
- Does your makeup seem to "melt away"?
- Do blemishes heal slowly or leave marks on your skin?

Dryness

- Are there scaling spots on your skin?
- Is your skin tight and mask-like after washing?
- Are there small lines around your eyes and mouth?
- Does your skin always seem "thirsty"?

If you've answered *yes* to most of the questions in any group, that section probably describes your skin. You might have dry and sensitive skin or oily and sensitive skin, or dry skin with a poor circulation, or even sagging oily skin (not all skin dries with age). If you know your own skin, it is easier for you to keep it in top condition.

THE PAPER SWATCH SKIN-TYPE TEST

If answering the questions above still hasn't specified your skin type, try this test.

Cut or tear a piece of plain white typing paper, or even brown paper from a paper bag, into five pieces. You can do this easily by folding the paper and then opening it up and cutting along the folds.

Label the pieces the following way:

- Forehead
- Nose
- Chin
- Right cheek
- Left cheek

For the test, wash your face carefully, then wait about two hours. Then, press the swatches to your forehead, nose, chin, and right and left cheeks. If any part of your face leaves a large oily spot on the paper, and it seems to become greasy, that section of your skin is probably oily. If it leaves no mark at all, that section of your skin is probably dry. Only a light, slightly moist mark should appear on any of the swatches. If you have the same condition on every part of your face, you are quite unusual. Most people don't have all dry skin or all oily skin, but combination skin. Even the oiliest complexions often suffer from dry skin around the eyes. Sometimes the skin is dry around the mouth, and near the temples, too. The oily part is the middle forehead, nose, and chin. This skin is not difficult to treat, but it does require more time than other skin types—often double the time.

Besides care at home, you'll need to continue your dual-ritual at work. You'll have to cleanse the oily sections of your skin by washing every four or five hours, and still protect the dry side. Do this by covering the dry sections with a light oil such as avocado oil before washing, and always use a moisturizer on the entire face. Blotting the oily sections with an astringent pad or cotton soaked in a mild astringent helps during the day.

But always examine your skin carefully to adjust your care to any changes due to the weather or your health. If your makeup looks fresh, you don't need to reapply during the day; however, if you do, be sure to protect the dry areas with oil or cream before washing, and moisturize after washing.

SKIN TYPES

Normal (clear): Healthy skin should be moist and soft to the touch; elastic and resilient. The skin surface should be slightly acid, and it should be healthy and firm, even in texture, tone, and color.

Less is more for your skin. Keep your skin at its perfect best by watching it carefully, following a healthy schedule, and warding off the ravages of aging by careful moisturizing and using lots of water both as rinses and compresses. An easy way to keep your skin looking perfect is by spraying it every few hours with a misty coating of water.

Dry: The advantage of dry skin is that it is usually small-pored and blemish-free. It is sometimes uncomfortable: tight feeling, itchy, and flaky. This type of skin is susceptible to small wrinkles and tiny lines.

Cleanse morning and night with a mild soap or with cream. Use lots of rinse water. Follow with a heavy application of moisturizer while the skin is still moist. A light coating of eye oil around the eyes should be used before any eye makeup. Avoid drafty spots because they tend to dry skin. And drink at least four glasses of water on the job every day.

Oily: The advantage of this skin type is that it ages slowly. It is shiny and greasy looking. The texture is coarse and open with large pores. The disadvantage is that the pores tend to clog, causing blemishes. Nerves and stress can stimulate oil glands and can cause blemishes, no matter how old you are. When you're feeling sticky and oily, just get up and wash your face. Keep astringent pads in your desk drawer for instant touch-ups.

Cleanse daily with a grainy scrub, followed by an antiseptic sealer or lotion to keep your skin clear. Wash your face during your lunch break; you can even use the strong detergent that is provided in many washrooms, but rinse carefully and apply moisturizer to your damp face before you reapply makeup. Oily skin care takes time, but the rewards will be fresh, youthful, blemish-free skin.

INDOOR/OUTDOOR WEATHER TIPS

Combination skin: Winter weather with icy temperatures and drying indoor heating will make the oily sections oilier, and the dry sections really dry. Try a night cream on the outer sides of your face, and switch from a light moisturizer to a heavier cream. Be sure your eyes and your neck are protected from harsh winds. Turtleneck blouses and sweaters are your skin's best friend.

Clear skin: Even the best skin can become dry and flaky in winter. Be sure a bowl of water or some very moist plant is near your work area on the job. If you notice your skin becoming red, rough, or chapped around the mouth, switch to dry skin care treatments.

Dry skin: You'll need all the protection you can get during cold weather, and if you live in a warm climate and work in an air-conditioned office, you'll have special problems. Use stick moisturizers, and chap-prevention methods. Keep your sunglasses ready to protect your eyes from squinting when out-of-doors, and be very careful to dab lotion or moisturizer on all exposed areas.

Oily skin: Remember to protect the eye area, your neck, and the backs of your hands when the weather gets cold. If you work outdoors, or spend much time traveling, you should consider modifying your daily skin care. Five daily face washings may be too many during cold spells.

Your skin is an organ, and there are four basic activities for caring for it: cleansing, stimulating, feeding, protecting.

CLEANSING

Probably the most repeated, the most important, and the most ignored beauty ritual is face washing. You do it every day; you've done it since childhood. But are you sure that you know the best way to wash your face?

A mild soap should be used for normal or dry skin, and a stronger one for cleaning the residue from oily skin.

First, wash your hands under running water. Use a nail brush if your nails are dirty.

With your fingertips, cover your face, except for the eye area and the neck, with vegetable oil. Dab the eye and neck area lightly with vegetable oil or lanolin.

Tissue off the excess oil and the cosmetics loosened by the oils by blotting with a tissue, not wiping.

Fill the basin with warm water for dry or delicate skin; if it is oily or troubled, use hot water.

With your hands, work the soap up into a bubbly lather. Using the fingertips of both hands, start at the base of the neck and, in a circular motion, work your hands up the sides of the neck. Use both hands so you are washing both sides of the face at the same time. Work as quickly as possible if your skin is dry. But oily skin responds well to a coating of bubbly suds—the lather acts as a masque.

The nose is often oily, and there may be large pores on it. This causes an accumulation of oil and dirt. Firmly clean the sides and the top of the nose.

Don't wash the sensitive eye area. It is too susceptible to dryness and wrinkling. The vegetable oil with the residue of eye makeup will be washed away with the rinsing. Any that is left can be removed with another application of vegetable oil.

Using the water in the basin, continue to rinse until your face feels clean and the last of the soap is washed away.

Rinse at least ten to twenty times. Your final rinse can be one of mineral water, distilled water, or a very weak solution of a half-cup of white vinegar to a half gallon of distilled water.

Then allow your face to evaporate dry, or apply your moisturizer to your wet-damp face. Or if you hate that drippy feeling, use paper toweling from the dispenser in the ladies' room to blot drops away gently.

The advantages of this method of face washing are many. You are not using cloths or brushes that introduce bacteria or microscopic particles to your skin. You are distorting the skin and underlying tissue as little as possible. And you are introducing as much moisture as possible to the surface of the skin.

STIMULATING

Exercise and *massage* are methods of stimulating and feeding the skin that will keep it feeling good as well as looking smooth. Just as a program of exercise is needed for a well-toned body, a regular program of skin exercise and stimulation is necessary for firm, supple skin tone and elasticity. Either facial massage, or toning masques, can be used to make your skin tight and radiant. A massage can be part of your daily at-work beauty routine.

You can develop your own special skin exercise program that can be practiced at home, in your car, or on the job. The only people who must be very careful not to overdo facial massage are those with very delicate skin that tends to develop broken capillaries or those with large-pored oily skin that attracts blemishes.

The massage will promote the active flow of sebaceous oils from sluggish glands and also increase the surface temperature and the flow of blood to the skin so that the nutrients will reach every cell of your skin.

Massage is a way of helping the skin heal itself. A facial massage can be done every lunch time, or coffee break, at your desk. This mini-massage can be done in less than a minute. The massage is done with the soft pad of the end of the middle finger. With this finger, it is easiest to exert just the right, gentle, firm, and even pressure.

But be cautious that you are applying pressure to the skin and underlying muscles, not just dragging at the skin layer. To do these exercises, clench your teeth and puff your cheeks.

Step 1: Place the middle fingers of both hands on your chin. Using small circular rotating motions, move your fingers up to the corners of your mouth, past the edges. Release; repeat three times.

Step 2: Place the fingers under the nostrils and stroke upward firmly on the outside of the nose, moving up toward the inner eye. Release; repeat twice.

Step 3: Using your fingers, start at the outer edge of the eye and massage upward toward the temple. When you reach the hairline, stop. Release; repeat twice.

Step 4: Using the middle fingers, press the muscle and skin of the bridge of the nose, urging it upward toward the top of your head with a circular motion. Release; repeat once.

These simple massages work doubly well when your face is creamed. And, if you change your makeup, these exercises performed on a clean face will prepare the skin for the moisturizer and your makeup will go on more smoothly since the exercises encourage a vigorous flow of blood to the skin surface.Follow the massages with an invigorating spray of cool water, or blot your entire face and neck with a paper towel, wrung out in cool water.

ASTRINGENTS AND SKIN FRESHENERS

There are hundreds of products that are sold as "toners" or facial "fresheners" and are thought to be stimulants for the skin. These lotions or liquids are usually mostly water with alcohol, and sometimes contain glycerin. The alcohol evaporates very quickly on the surface of the skin and makes it feel cool, tight, and refreshed. The glycerin helps the lotion to spread evenly and to leave a finished surface on the skin. Overuse of astringents can be drying and you should avoid using them near your eyes. There is no evidence that they actually help to "shrink" pores.

At work, astringents can help to rid the skin of old makeup (the water and alcohol are super cleansers) and can make you feel fresh and alive. But many strip the skin of natural oils, and you should follow any astringent with a moisturizer.

The best astringents leave the skin slightly acid, and you can use a mixture of water and lemon juice sealed in a sterile glass jar. (To sterilize a glass jar boil it in water for about 10 minutes.)

PROTECTING

Your skin replenishes itself every twenty-six to thirty-three days. This means that in a few short weeks, it will show the effects of the treatment you are giving it now.

No matter how perfect your features are, no matter how symmetrical their shape and how exquisite their proportion, you cannot look your best unless your skin is smooth and blemish-free. Working brings a variety of problems, and the skin responds to these problems. The color, size, and function of other organs are influenced by heredity, and so is the skin. But the skin, more than any other organ, immediately reflects the emotions and health. And it depends on constant grooming and care for maintaining its function. The skin, unlike other organs, is constantly replenishing itself. You can help some of the following problem areas with some amazingly simple solutions. Blotchy skin, for example.

Working late, anger, too many coffee breaks, and a myriad of other events can bring blotchy skin. If you have red, angry patches on your skin, or if sections of your skin seem almost covered with raised marks, you may be using something on your face that is causing a chemical burn. Strong acids and alkalis in some cosmetics, soaps, and skin aids can cause chemical burns. These discolored areas should be treated in a way similar to the way you might treat other burns: Wash often with cool water and avoid infections.

Splotches, scaly or itching spots, and other allergic reactions can be caused by a sensitive reaction to pollen or air pollution, food, or certain cosmetics. If you suspect that you might have a skin allergy from a cosmetic, avoid it for a few days. Wash often using only water. If your skin improves, you'll know that that cosmetic isn't for you. Try another and another—until you find one that won't cause the allergic reaction.

Red splotches can also be the result of a sudden flush or change in the blood's circulation. If you have very thin skin (skin, just as height and weight, varies considerably), a very exciting or stressful situation might raise your temperature slightly and make your skin flush. This flushing is not good and can cause long-term skin damage in the form of broken blood vessels. The thin-skinned should never alternate hot and cold face washes or rinses. And don't treat a flushed face with ice cubes, but gently lower the skin's temperature and restore the normal circulation with warm, cool, then cooler water rinses.

Emotions can have almost immediate reactions on your skin. Bad news has been known to give some women acne in a few hours. Excitement, stress, lack of sleep, worry, and even joy can equally affect skin.

A good cry may make you feel better. But after the first flush of crying, your skin may appear dead and dry. So try a masque—a creamy one if you have dry skin, and if you have oily skin, a pore-tightening one. Lie down for about fifteen minutes and put a witchhazel-soaked or water-soaked cotton pad or a cloth on your face, a cucumber slice over each eye, and soothing music on the radio.

Once you are feeling better, restore your makeup. A dark eyeshadow on the lid will usually cover the redness. Smudged gray or brown eyeliner will also help. A thin eye-whitening line of blue eye pencil on the inner rim of the lid will make your eyes look less red and bloodshot. And a bright lipstick will call attention to your mouth rather than to your eyes.

Your skin will change often—the weather, sleep, stress, and other internal and external elements affect skin. To cope with changes, be vigilant at all times. Inspect your skin carefully every day in a well-lighted mirror. Don't just look at one feature or the other when applying makeup. Take in the entire face.

Some jobs can be harmful to your skin. There are hazards in every occupation, but some special problems await the workers in the following jobs:

Airline attendant: Dry skin may result from the dry air in the cabins, and vascular problems such as varicose veins may occur from the pressurized take-offs and landings.

Hairdressers: Exposure to harsh chemicals such as peroxide and dye. The chemicals sometimes are carried to the face, unless a worker is careful. Workers should wear gloves as often as possible.

Dancers and athletes: If you are in a dance studio or gym or sauna you can contract skin and fungus diseases. The dried perspiration and the dampness is a perfect place for bacteria to grow. Women athletes, coaches, locker workers, and dancers should carefully check their skin, and cover even the smallest scratch with a bandage. Dancers' feet need special care.

Nurses and dental workers: Obviously have your hands near trouble much of the time. Wash often, dry carefully, and moisturize often.

Laboratory technicians: Often exposed to chemicals and

must be careful to avoid contamination from their work.

Switchboard operators and people who work on the telephone: Clean your mouthpiece often, but be sure you don't leave any residue of the cleaner on it. Rubbing the mouthpiece against the sensitive skin of your lips or chin can cause blisters and problems. Cradling the phone between your jaw and shoulder for an extended conversation can lead to a tension headache, as well as a raspy throat. Don't hesitate to request a lightweight mouthpiece if you talk on the phone more than an hour a day.

Teachers: Children often cough and sneeze without care, and they can also be quite violent. (I bear the scars of an unhappy child who was unable to express himself and bit my hand when I attempted to give him some paints.)

Insomnia, or insufficient sleep, for example, can cause your skin to be lackluster, dull, and drab. It can delay the healing of minor blemishes and encourage small infections. Part of a total skin-care program is to get the sleep you need to function the following day. To get sufficient sleep, make sure that you exercise before going to bed, and then relax with a half cup of low-fat yogurt.

Premenstrual problems: The monthly change of hormonal balance can play havoc with your skin.

It brings about skin eruptions and often an accumulation of fluid that can distort your skin and features. Your eyes can become puffy, your skin lackluster.

To cut down on these premenstrual problems:

A week or two before your period avoid salty foods, drink an extra glass of pure water each day, and use warm tea bags on your eyes to reduce the puffiness.

Menstrual cramps: These painful cramps and the dehydration that sometimes accompanies them can be reduced by medication that has just been approved by the Food and Drug Administration. It retards the production of protaglandins, the body chemicals that cause cramping.

Just as you change your wardrobe to protect your body from the weather, you should be changing your skin care. Every winter, the skin of your face goes from below zero to hot, dry, heated rooms, and outdoors again. In the summer, it puts up with drying sun and wind, and sometimes temperature that is above body level.

To guard against winter's ravages, you'll need moisturizers and bath oils. A moisturizer, covered with a thin coat of petroleum jelly, will protect your skin from the evaporation of moisture in temperatures that go below zero.

Summer, winter, spring, or fall, moist skin glowing with health and with a smooth satin finish is the best. Keeping your skin moist and healthy in any season can be accomplished by drinking at least eight glasses of water a day besides the liquid that you drink in coffee or other drinks. Use lots of water when you wash and rinse your face. Protect your own natural moisture from evaporating by using moisturizers and lotions.

For your summer skin care, wear sunglasses to protect the thin skin around your eyes from the drying heat and rays of the sun and to help you avoid squinting and forming wrinkles. If you're bothered with whiteheads or small cysts caused by over-production of oil in the summer months, frequently use washing grains.

Sun can be your skin's worst enemy. No matter what your complexion, the sun is aging (for older women with light skin, it is most damaging). And if you are taking tranquilizers, diuretics, or estrogen drug/hormone, or are a diabetic you run the risk of an infection resulting from any small burn blister that you may get. This is especially true of people who work indoors all year and attempt to tan quickly over a week or even a weekend.

Always begin your tan slowly; twenty minutes on the first day in temperate zones is quite enough. And be very careful of your shoulders, knees, tops of feet, lips, and ears, as these areas are most sensitive to burning. Remember that a summer of dark tanning may be followed by a winter of dry raspy skin and aging wrinkles. Use a sunscreen lotion. If you get a sunburn accompanied by chills or a fever, see a doctor. If your skin turns an uncomfortable red, soothe it with talcum powder. If you have a burn, apply wet dressings of gauze dipped in a solution of baking soda and cornstarch which has been mixed with cool water or milk. If you work outdoors, always wear sunscreen makeup on the job for protection.

Never wear perfume when you go into the sun. A complex

interplay of body chemistry often causes the perfume to form brown spots on the skin which last a long time and can mar your complexion for months.

Just as you would inspect your clothing for wear, a spot, or a stain, or to see that it is well-pressed and lint-free, get in the habit of inspecting your skin—and really notice its reaction to makeup, treatments, and cleansing preparations.

FEEDING

You can feed your skin best with water. Without water the nutrients in your food are less effective, with 10 to 12 glasses a day you will notice an improvement in about a week. More about feeding in the chapter on nutrition.

FACIAL EXERCISES TO DO AT YOUR DESK

Just as your body needs exercise, so does your face. Take your eyes, for example.

Eye contact means communication, and it is very important in working with other people. Your eyes should be clear and sparkling when this happens. And they can be if you exercise them at your desk. If your eyes are bloodshot, just a few moments of exercise in combination with eyedrops will overcome "conference room" eyes. Do these exercises without your glasses, if you usually wear them.

Follow a moving object with both eyes. Watch someone come toward you or move away. Next, try to focus on an object as far away as possible.

Pick an object to your left and one to your right. Without moving your head, look as far to your left and then as far to your right as possible. Repeat the same exercise looking at a point on the ceiling and one on the floor.

Changing the focus of your eyes is very important, especially if you do close work, such as laboratory, clerical, or detailed handwork. Try to get a few minutes outdoors every day—just to change your field of focus. Focus as far away as possible; it is restful for eyes that do too much close-up work.

Exercise twice a day, or any time your eyes feel achy or tired.

You can massage your eyes, too. Close your eyes and place the pads of your fingertips over the outer corners of your eyes and, using a gentle circular motion, just press gently against the eyeball. After a few moments, replace the fingers to the inner corners of the eye, near the nose, and repeat the exercise.

Another method of relaxing your eyes is simply to cover them with your palms or the heels of your hands. Shut out all light so that if you open your eyes you will stare at darkness. This will help to exercise the iris and your entire eye.

The following facial wrinkle-fighting exercises are easy enough to do at your desk, but they might cause some comment, as they involve a great deal of facial motion. These wrinkle-fighting exercises have two functions: They strengthen the muscles beneath the skin and bring circulation to the skin, and they also seem to relax the muscles that might be tense because of stress and are therefore often useful to rid yourself of a headache.

Neck: Thrust your lower jaw forward, keeping your mouth open and tensing your neck so the muscles are all stretched.

Cheeks: Keep them round and firm by placing your hands on either side of your face. Rest the tip of your third finger on the top of your cheekbones. Hold the sides of your face firmly and then wrinkle your nose by trying to move it back, and curl your upper lip.

Forehead: Place your index fingers on your eyebrows. Hold them firmly with the sides of the fingers. Try to move your brows up—but make your fingers resist the movement.

Mouth: Place your hands over the jaws just in front of the earlobes. Press, and at the same time clench your teeth together, smiling as broadly as possible.

Yawn, stretching your neck, and at the same time try to touch your elbows together behind your back. This general movement is good for your overall circulation. With vigorous circulation, your own blood supply will keep your body—muscles and brain—well-fortified with life-giving oxygen and cell-building nutrients.

On-the-Job Makeup

In the fall of 1936, an article entitled "Vanity or Sanity" appeared in a well-known magazine. The article explained how the loss of interest in personal fashion, grooming, and cosmetics is a health signal that should not be ignored. Yet nearly half a century later, we are still suspicious of cosmetics. It is only the new emphasis on keeping fit and the amazing computer-generated advances in makeup formulation that finally have forced us to accept the therapeutic advantages of cosmetics.

The products, techniques, and expert advice once possible only for the rich and leisured now are available to everyone. And it is the rich who are actually turning into working women—many of whom are devoted to bringing the best in beauty to their sisters. The $6 to $7 billion makeup industry shows no sign of slow-down no matter what inflation or under-employment might mean to other industries.

WHAT YOU SHOULD KNOW ABOUT COSMETICS

A careful and expert makeup is an important credential for any applicant, as has been shown in Chapter 1, when the job interview was discussed. Sitting across a desk, about four feet from the interviewer, your ability to use cosmetics will show your personal self-confidence, attention to detail, social awareness, ability to select appropriate solutions for a problem, and your interest in getting the job.

The law defines a cosmetic as a substance that is intended to be rubbed, poured, sprinkled, or sprayed on, introduced onto, or applied to the human body for cleansing, beautifying, and/or promoting attractiveness, or changing the appearance in any way.

So when you're buying or using cosmetics, here are eleven safety rules to remember:

1. Read cosmetic labels carefully and follow directions exactly. (Later, when you know your reaction, you can experiment—hand cream can be used as face cream; shadow as blusher; eye pencils as lip liners.)
2. To test for allergy to a cosmetic, apply a small amount to the inside of your forearm and leave it there for twenty-four hours. Check for redness and blisters. Also check your eyes: Are they more bloodshot than usual? Do they itch? These are both signs of allergic reactions.
3. *Hypoallergenic* means *less* likelihood of allergic reaction.
4. If a cosmetic causes any adverse effect—burning, "breaking out," stinging, or itching—stop using it. If you see a doctor, take the cosmetic with you.
5. Wash your hands before applying a cosmetic.
6. Close containers after each use.
7. Never use another person's cosmetics.
8. Never use saliva to moisten a cosmetic.
9. Don't expect the impossible; a cosmetic cannot change your life or get you the promotion, but it may give you self-confidence.
10. Don't expect a cosmetic to be a cure.
11. Throw old cosmetics away; be ruthless.

Some products are equally suitable for different effects. If a product is suitable as an eyeshadow, it can also be used as a blusher. If a product is described as a facial moisturizer or cream, it can also be used as a body cream. Enamels and manicure tools are equally good on toes and fingers. Exceptions include products that are not intended for the eyes or lips.

You can mix brand products whenever you wish. The manufacturer makes suggested groupings, but don't hesitate to mix and match.

PERFECTING THE LOOK OF YOUR SKIN

Your makeup cannot be perfect unless your skin is perfect. Few women have perfect skin all the time. But makeup can enhance the illusion of perfection while covering or minimizing flaws; and the new makeups can actually help to correct skin problems as you wear them.

Whether your skin is oily, combination, or dry, or if it is clear or uneven toned, there is a makeup or a combination of makeups for you. Science, medicine, and cosmetology have recently combined—sometimes with the aid of a computer—to provide a vast array of skin-loving products. Read the label carefully when you buy cosmetics. Question the beauty consultant or salesperson about any ingredients that seem unusual. Would you buy a pair of shoes without checking them for size, width, and fit? Then buy only a small size of all cosmetics and test them for "fit" to your skin.

Moisturizers

To give your makeup the best possible surface, cleanse your face thoroughly. While your skin is wet, smooth on a moisturizer. Use it around your eyes, on your neck, and the backs of your hands. If your face is very oily, skip your nose, and other areas that might be blemish-prone.

If you use a water-base foundation that is developed just for oily skin, don't use a moisturizer under it. A toner (to even out your complexion) might be better for your skin type.

Too much moisturizer or a product that is not compatible with the acid-alkaline surface of your skin can cause "vanishing makeup." This occurs when you put makeup on in the morning, but by noon it is gone, faded, turned a different shade, has smudged, or just seems dull and caked.

To combat this, you might want to try several different types of moisturizer and see which works best for you. Generally, the more liquid the product, the lighter the consistency and the less oily. A very dry skin might need a thick, creamy moisturizer that is almost solid; an oily skin or oily parts of the skin respond well to thin liquids. Here is a tip for getting your moisturizer to combine with your skin, forming a base for your foundation, not combining with the foundation and melting away the color.

- Wring a damp cloth or natural sponge in warm water.
- Blot face.
- Apply moisturizer to the damp face.
- Apply the foundation.
- Blot with damp cloth or sponge again.

Whether your makeup is water- or oil-based, it should last longer on the skin if you do this. This is also a good, quick midday pickup for your makeup.

Concealers

Study your clean, fresh, just-moisturized face. Do you have dark circles under the eyes, deep lines, or shadows around your mouth, or noticeable skin flaws such as discolored marks, pimples, or birthmarks? Or are there some features of your face you would like to minimize or reshape?

This is the time to use an under-makeup concealer, available in sticks, tubes, and pencils. For uneven skin tone, you might want to use two or three different makeup foundation colors rather than the thicker and more opaque sticks. George Masters, the famous Hollywood beauty consultant, suggests a creamy light concealer applied with a sable brush to keep it from clogging or creping.

Many women like to prepare a bit of their own makeup color combined with the concealer in a small plastic makeup case for easy use. One of the mistakes that people make is to put makeup over the concealer, and then blend. In this way, the concealer is often vigorously blended all over the face.

Match the concealer shade as closely as you can to your skin color for the most effective and subtle application. Use a shade of concealer that is only one shade lighter than your skin for deep lines or discolorations like blemishes or birthmarks. If you use a concealer that is too light, it will bring these flaws to attention.

In places where you blend the concealer and your makeup, tap the two together lightly using the fleshy pads of your fingertips.

If you have oily skin and you want to conceal a blemish, don't use an oily stick concealer. First dab the blemish with an antiseptic, such as witchhazel or astringent, or a bit of water-based makeup. Be sure that the makeup doesn't build up or cake, and then cover the rest of the face with the makeup foundation. Tap the two areas together.

Foundations

Every woman who is old enough to work is old enough to wear makeup and should wear it so that she always looks her best. If you work in a restaurant, factory, or in an air conditioned office, it is vital for the health of your skin to protect it. If you work outdoors, makeup can be your shield and safeguard against windburn, sunspots, and skin aging.

Foundations enhance skin tone, dramatize coloring, and make you look healthier and more alert. If your skin tone needs correcting because it has too much yellow—making you look sallow—or if it has too much pink, making you look flushed and excited, it may give a false impression of your emotional state. Women have made great strides, but there is always someone in every office who likes to think that women are psychologically unsuited for stress or business responsibilities and the high salaries that go with them. Don't give them any excuse.

There are at least several thousand makeups. Hundreds are available to almost everyone. Every manufacturer makes at least four or five shades, and usually those shades come in a variety of consistencies. They can be liquids, creams, salves, sticks, pencils, gels, or cakes. You want a shade and color that look natural with your skin. It doesn't have to blend with your skin—in fact, it can be a slightly different tone—but it should look natural.

If your skin surface is shiny and oily, it is only reasonable to avoid emollients that are dewy, moist, and feel oily when they go on. If your skin is flaky or tends to dry and crack, it is obvious that you want a moist, oily makeup and that a water-based makeup will just leave you with parched skin.

Your makeup-foundation wardrobe should include several foundations:

Oily skin: Water-based makeup for nose, cheeks, and chin; oil-based in the same shade for eyes, neck, and outer cheeks.

Combination skin: Water-based for nose; oil-based for cheeks, neck, chin; lightweight thin oil-based makeup for eye area, as it tends to wrinkle.

Dry skin: Oil-based makeup in cream or stick for longer coverage and most protection; thin oil-based liquid foundation for eye and neck area, and around mouth.

The trend for work-wear coverage is light matte that stays on at least eight hours. Gels give the lightest coverage and are most natural, but they will leave you with an unfinished look not suitable for a formal office. Look for makeups that are described as "long-wearing" or "waterproof," or try makeups that are designed for "all-weather" or "outdoor" wear; these are formulated to stay put. If your makeup changes color or the effect lasts less than three hours, discard the makeup and try another brand. Experiment and try brands that are designed for stage makeup if you cannot find a durable brand in commercial outlets. Or write to such companies as Max Factor, who are interested in the durability of their makeup, and you'll get topflight beauty advice from their specialists.

Just as makeup comes in many textures, their colors also vary tremendously. There are only a few rules to remember in selecting the right color.

Go lighter or darker than your own skin tone by only one or two shades.

Avoid shades that are too rosy. Instead, warm up your face with a blusher. Too rosy shades leave a noticeable demarcation line between your chin and neck.

Unless you have a very rosy complexion or a suntan, use a beige shade for office wear.

Women get into patterns of applying their face makeup and actually don't realize that they probably do the same thing over and over. If you have a habit, be sure that it is a good one. The most important habit is using a light touch. Don't pull your skin as you apply makeup. If you can't get the makeup on evenly without stretching your skin with your fingertips, use a water-soaked sponge. Using your facial muscles, stiffen your face so that your skin is resting on a firm surface as you glide the makeup foundation or press pencils over your skin.

In the delicate eye area, work all the creams and makeups from the outer corner toward the inner corner. Work the cheek areas upward and outward toward the temples, and work any creams or makeup on the neck upward and toward the ears.

There is no rule that you have to use only one color foundation on your face at any one time. You can use any combination of shades and textures. A narrow face might look best with a slightly lighter shade used on the cheeks and jaw. The lighter shade may make the jaw look stronger. Conversely, a rounded face, or one with a squarish jaw, might look best with a slightly darker shade of the same makeup foundation spread on the outer edges of the jaw. Blend all the edges carefully.

Powder

Consider the kind of finish that will best fit your working image. If you want a soft matte finish, cover the makeup foundation with a heavy dusting of powder, then dust it off with a light brush. A good coating of powder will help your makeup set properly and stay clean-looking and fresh longer.

Loose powder provides a velvet finish that cannot be duplicated by pressed powder. If your skin is oily, there are oil-absorbing powders that will actually help to prevent your makeup from turning off-color or melting.

For dry or maturing skin, the powder may cake or sink into small lines. So if you have dry skin be very careful to rid your face of any excess powder.

Translucent powder finishes makeup without adding color. All skin tones and shades can wear translucent powder well. And if you have used concealer and several different makeup base shades, a translucent powder will help to blend them together visually.

To apply face powder, use a brush, a puff, or a cotton swab. Whisk the brush across your face, and then pat and press with the cotton if you use both. Don't worry about using too much powder; apply it liberally and then brush off the excess with a dry, clean brush or a light pass with cotton or the puff. Some people like feather puffs, or even puffs made of lamb's wool, similar to the kind used on stage. You'll have to develop the methods that work best for you.

Blush

Powder blush goes on next to give your face color. The powder form gives a soft matte effect that covers glossy highlights that are common if your face is oily or has large pores. If you have small-pored dry skin, or work in a drying atmosphere, such as a heated or an air-conditioned room, use a cream or gel blush.

If you use a powder blush in the morning, you can touch it up with a cream blush after lunch, or when your makeup starts to fade. If your skin is very dry, don't cover the gel or cream with powder. The slight moist shine will give you a softer, more youthful look.

In applying a blush, the best technique is to blend it over the cheekbones and toward the hairline. But you can also use the blush for sculpting, and here is how:

A high, wide forehead: Make your jaw stronger by blending blush down toward your earlobe.

Too prominent chin: Draw attention to the upper part of

Face Shapes

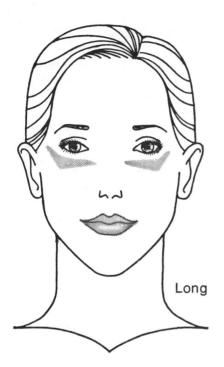

Long

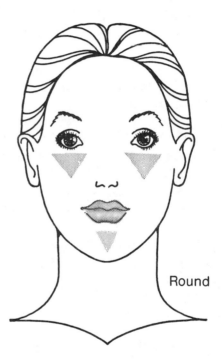

Round

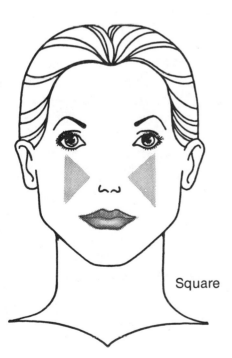

Square

the face by bringing the blush up and around the outer corner of the eye and across the forehead.

Too wide nose: Slightly shade the sides of the nose.

One of the latest techniques used by many cosmetic designers is to bring the blusher up around the eye area. It seems to bring a lift and sparkle to even a tired eye.

Blusher can be used to change the shape of your face or enhance it. Take a look at the form face shapes below:

Long Face: The old expression, "Don't make a long face!" comes from the fact that this shape makes the owner look sad. A long face is often narrow, so you should create a shorter and wider illusion. Keep everything from the mid-cheek area to the temple and outside of the face. Keep your eyebrows straight; wear glasses with horizontal frames, and keep your eyeshadow outward. The blusher should be used in a very narrow horizontal V under the eye, and then a wing is added up toward the eye. Your lips should be slightly extended.

Round face: The round face has a soft and youthful look. Make the most of this, but give some character to your face by defining the cheekbones. With the blusher, make a triangular shape with the wide part under the eye. The narrow tip ends just under the cheekbone. Strengthen other features while still keeping the softness of your round face. Taper the brows upward. Do just the opposite of what is done for the long face. With the round face, all lines should go up and down. Avoid horizontal lines. Shadow and rouge should bring the eye upward. Keep the shape of your mouth full and round. Make a delicate downward pointing arrow of rouge on the chin to lengthen it.

Square face: This angular shape needs softening. So make your jaw look rounder and perhaps even more smoothly delicate by arching the eyebrows and bringing attention away from the outer edges. Angle the brows with a peak to lift the eye area. Find the center of your eye. Now draw a triangle to cover the lower cheek, spreading from the nose toward the ear in a rough triangle with the narrowest point to the eye. Bring some interest to your mouth. A bright lipstick, for example, will draw attention away from the cheeks to the center of your face.

Experiment with shapes and color. No one can tell you what is right for you all the time. The ideas here are only directions, or guideposts.

Now look to the final touches: lips and eyes. Emphasizing these features will give personality to your face. But call attention to one or the other of these features, not both.

LIPS

When you greet people, talk, or participate in discussions with co-workers, your mouth is as important as your eyes in conveying your abilities and attracting attention. Your breath, teeth, and the tone and range of your vocal chords will all contribute to the effect of your lipstick or lip color. Before you speak, your lips should be picture perfect.

There are many new lip products on the market. The variety of techniques and products mean that you can have the lips that look best and are most comfortable for you.

Lip pencils are new. Learn to use them, because they are convenient for touch-ups when a brush might be difficult. Lip pencils are best for reshaping your mouth. If you think your lips should be thinner, draw the lip line just inside the edge of the natural line. For a fuller look, draw the line on the outer edge. Don't draw a shape that is drastically different from your own. It will look artificial and will not stay. Lip color will naturally smear toward your natural shape. The best method is to play up what you do have. Darker edges and lighter lip centers make your lips look fuller.

For long-lasting color, use a tube lipstick. Be sure that the color glides on evenly. Throw out old lipsticks, and try to get the freshest product you can. A year-old lipstick is like a dried-out crayon.

Create your own lip gels by mixing a tube lipstick with petroleum jelly. Put about a half-inch of the lipstick in a tiny glass container (the kind used for cosmetic samples) and add about a teaspoon of petroleum jelly. Mix them together with a small stick, and then cap for later use. Gels have less coverage and color than other forms of lipstick, but they are wonderful because they prevent dry-outs and can be used over, under, with, and without any other form of lip color.

When you want super shine and a gleamy romantic glint that is completely compatible with office wear, you should try the new lip colors that are applied with sponge-tip wands.

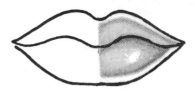

Thick

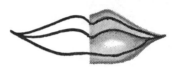

Thin

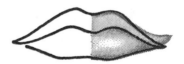

Drooping

Chapped

To disguise small imperfections so that your mouth seems in perfect proportion and fits your all-over face shape, try some of the following methods:

Uneven lips: These can be evened up by carefully outlining one section to build it up while diminishing the other. By doing this, you can make the width of the upper and lower lips the same at the fullest point, and the right and left sides of your mouth as close to identical as possible.

Thick lips: Lips that are thick will look less full if you apply a coat of foundation over the entire lip area. Then, using a pencil one shade darker than the lipstick you will use, draw your lip outline just inside the natural edge. Powder your lips inside this drawn area, and you'll keep the color in place.

Thin lips: Lips that are thin are treated in the opposite way. Apply the foundation. Outline just beyond the natural line with the pencil. Fill in carefully. Tissue blot. Then, using a lip brush, even out the color once again. Put gloss on the center of the lips to give them a soft, full look.

Drooping, downturned lips: These can give a hard, unattractive expression. They can be corrected by painting the tiny upper edges of the outer corners of the mouth with a heavy foundation or a concealer stick. Then, using a pencil, raise the outer lip line slightly at the corners. The line should be an upward extension of your lower lip. Fill in with a lip pencil.

Chapped, cracked lips: Lips such as these need a coating of gloss, or a product like Chapstick.

Puckered, aging lips: Aging lips will require stretching the skin with one hand as you carefully apply the lipstick with the other. Don't use a greasy lipstick, or a lip gloss, which will "feather" out from the creases.

EYES

At work, just as in social situations, your eyes tell all. For a pair that will look calm, clear, and effective—mirroring your well-organized mind—you'll need: tweezers, eyebrow pencils, a small soft brush and/or comb, a sharpener, and eye pencils, powders, or creams in colors that compliment your eyes.

Choose a brow color that will make your eyebrows as near in color to your scalp hair as possible. Don't draw a single continuous line to shape your brows, but use short feathery strokes, or gather color on your brush from the pencil and brush it onto your brows. Short strokes with a pencil or powder applied with a brush give the most natural effect.

Your eyebrows should start directly above the inner corner of your eye. Then they should arch over the center of your eye (farther to the outside if your eyes are too close-set), and extend to the outer corner of your eye.

New eyeshadow colors and effects are created every day. But every new look is not for everyone; some eye makeups are definitely not for work-wear. A combination of a light oil, such as avocado oil or another vegetable oil, with just a bit of powdered shadow on it, works well for most businesswomen, as it puts less stress on the delicate eyelid skin. The light oil protects the lids and underbrow area, and forms a perfect base. If, however, your powder creeps into the crease between the lid and your brow area, you are using too much oil.

A few general pointers to consider in application of eyeshadow colors are as follows.

The shadow color should blend with your makeup and costume. Don't match your shadow to your eye color—contrast the

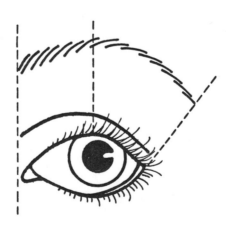

Eye Shape

color of your eye with the area around it. It will make your eye color look more intense.

Prominent eyes: The more prominent (even bulgy) your eyes, the more subdued your shadow colors should be. Use soft colors over the lids and extend the color up the lids to the crease and over the eye bone. But use highlighting shades very sparingly.

Deep-set eyes: Use a clean sharp color to enlarge them. Apply highlights (that are lighter than skin tones) lavishly. Deep-set eyes can be mysterious and haunting. Put a darker shadow in the eye crease and blend it at the outer corner. Use a light color beneath the brow bone. Use mascara on the outer lashes, both top and bottom.

Almond eyes: Slightly tilted and wide-set, considered the ideal shape. Play up the feature by applying color over the entire lid and under the eye on the lower lid, too. Use mascara and liner to call attention to your eye shape.

Narrow-lidded eyes: Often a feature of Oriental and black women. Your eyes look exotic and intense; but you'll need to create the illusion of a deeper lid. Do this by drawing a line from the inner corner of the eye just under the brow and around onto the crease between the lids and the brow bone. Smudge and blend. Keep the mascara on the upper lids only.

Down-tilted eyes: When the inner corners of the eyes are higher than the outer corners, the eyes have the look of continual questioning or tragedy. Using a pencil or liquid liner, draw a line from the upper lid outward and slightly upward. Extend the line beyond the outer corner of the eye. Smudge that line upward, and use shadow color only above that line. Keep your mascara only on the center and inner lashes.

Wide-set eyes: Give the face a flat expression. This is most evident if you've had your nose changed through plastic surgery. Jackie O., who avoids all eye makeup, is very aware that her eyes are too far apart and too small. She overcomes this by calling attention away from her eyes to her mouth. If you wear eye makeup, the focus of attention should be on the inner corners of the eye. Apply mascara heavily to the inner lashes, both top and bottom. Start near the nose bridge.

Close-set eyes: Accent the outer corners to make eyes appear farther apart. Use heavier color, and more mascara on the outer edge.

Bags or circles beneath the eyes: One of the all time eye

problems. To correct this, you'll need a very soft sable brush or a cotton swab. Use heavy color above the eye, and if the circles are exceptionally dark, use a bit more blusher.

The dark line at the bottom of the circle should be delicately painted with a light or reflective white color. Put the color on, starting at the inner corner under the eye, then move downward and around the bottom of the circle, just at the edge of the eye socket. Don't use your fingertip. You can get a finer, smoother, lighter, and less skin-pulling effect when you use a brush. Do not put the light color near the puffy section of the "bag."

Mascara

A very thick, but non-beaded application of mascara can make almost any woman look more feminine and attractive. Mascara is available in browns, blacks, and greys. It also can be found in cake form, wand form, and even in long-lasting dyes. Some mascaras are mixed with tiny fibers that adhere to the lashes and make them look thicker.

Consider your needs and how often you'll be touching up your makeup. Choose a waterproof mascara if you wash your face during the day, or if you are in a moist or warm climate. Don't stroke the applicator from base to tip of the lashes. Twirl, wiggle, and move the applicator vertically *from side to side.* You can get more color on the lashes in that way. If you're going to apply more than one coat, allow time to dry between coats, and powder the lashes between coats.

If you have problems with smudging and smearing mascara, give the lashes plenty of time to dry before you blink your eyes. Check your eyes with and without mascara. If your eyes itch, ache, or tear with the mascara on, discard that brand and try another. You are having an allergic reaction.

MAKEUP COLORS

Keeping in color fashion is very important for a working woman. Old-fashioned colors give you an old, staid look, and reflect unfavorably on you and your general ability. Here are some of the colors that are waning in popularity, and some that are growing. The trend to the 1980s is easy to see:

	More popular	**Less popular**
Eye shadow	brown, gray, violet, pink	blue, green, beige
Lipstick	mocha, cinnamon, coral	red, pink, light melon shades
Nail enamel	mocha, spice, wines	red, pink, corals
Mascara	black, wine, brown	blue, metallic

The best, most elegant chic looks are those in which all the color accents—clothing, accessories, makeup—blend together. They should not be matched for a stiff contrived look, but should all follow a monochromatic "family" feeling.

To save time and trouble you should separate your make-ups into two or three groups in a small box or in three plastic bags. Group the makeups that will perfectly complement your daily color scheme. Here is a good, easy way to do this. Think of the colors of your garments, accessories, etc., in the following way:

- *Neutrals:* deep brown, gray, black, white, clear red
- *Sky tones:* blues, pinks, rose, wine, purple
- *Earth tones:* peach, coral, orange, greens, umbers, camels, clay, spices, beige

With the neutrals—for example, a gray outfit—you can wear a makeup keyed to either sky or earth tones. With an avocado-green outfit, you might want to play up the earth tones. You can do this very easily by keeping a set of makeup colors—a shadow, lipstick, eyebrow pencil, and blusher—in a small plastic bag (a sandwich bag is just about the right size). If you have two bags, labeled "Sky Colors" and "Earth Colors," you can then select the right palette for your outfit and carry the makeup with you easily and conveniently in your handbag.

Color in makeup can work for you, but it needs planning, organization, and then follow-through. All the cosmetics in the world, unused, or used incorrectly, will not help. Proficiency is a matter of use, training, and attention to detail.

FIFTEEN-MINUTE MAKEUP

This is how you can apply your makeup in just fifteen minutes. The directions here are for a complete re-do that can be accomplished in the morning before rushing to work, in the ladies' room at the office, or when you have to look your very best—morning, noon, or night—for some special occasion. But note: This makeup routine will only work when a weekly program of beauty care for a total look of good grooming is followed. So set your clock and follow along. You might be able to beat the fifteen-minute time:

TIME
(min.)

	Start with a sparkling clean face.
2	Dot the face with a moisturizer—forehead, cheeks, mouth, and chin; even out the moisturizer, dotting it carefully under the eyes.
2	To even out the skin tone, dot a liquid foundation over the moisturizer and carefully blend.
2	If you use a blemish cover, or a sculpture-color to create the illusion of perfect features, apply and blend carefully. (Some prefer this step before applying the foundation.)
½	Apply your rouge, cheek color, or blusher.
1	Draw an eyeline—in liquid with a brush (small and carefully cut down), or with a pencil or crayon—above the upper lids near the lashes. Unless you are a dark brunette or black woman, avoid a single straight line. Dot the color on, keeping it soft and subtle.
2	Now comes the eyeshadow. Remember: Don't use a color that matches the color of your eyes; use a color that contrasts. It doesn't even have to match the color of your dress or anything else. Your eyeshadow should be selected because it makes your eyes look best.
1	Using a large soft brush or a bit of cotton, fluff loose powder over your entire face. Even out the powder, being sure it doesn't get into your hair or become clogged in the small hairs at the sides of your face. Always apply mascara after powder—the flakes of powder thicken your lashes.
1	Brush mascara on both your upper and lower eyelashes. Brush and brush again. Move the brush horizontally across the tips of the lashes, both upper and lower.
1	Check the effect; clean up any small mistakes; add more blusher if needed, even out mascara, and so on.
2	Your lips should be covered with foundation and powder. Using

a lip brush or one of the new small sponge applicators, carefully shape your upper lip outline, and then the lower lip outline. Don't blot.

½   Cover the lip color with gloss. Touch up any details with a sharp lip pencil, if needed.

Did you do it all in fifteen minutes? Well, with a little practice, you soon will.

YOUR OFFICE BEAUTY KIT

Very few women feel perfectly made-up and groomed all day. Most need some sort of remake, or at least touching up.

For this, you should assemble a desk drawer beauty kit to leave at work. The problem is keeping it all together, leak-free, and clean. One of the neatest looking and best cases you can use is a series of zippered pencil cases held in a small three-ring binder which gives you a set of neat waterproof bags where your hair, skin, or cosmetic-care products can be held in separate containers.

Some other things you can use are plastic bags, aluminum foil, etc.; a man's large handkerchief folded Japanese-style (knot alternate ends together); children's plastic pencil cases; small paper or wooden boxes. Don't walk from your desk to the ladies' room carrying a flowered or obvious makeup case; it reinforces false stereotypes of women being vain.

These are some of the beauty-care items you might consider keeping at your desk.

- Toothpaste
- Toothbrush
- Dental floss or toothpicks
- Mouthwash
- Hand cream
- Moisturizer
- Cleansing pads (especially good when it's hot and humid)
- Face blotters–a blotting product for absorbing old makeup and for oily skin
- An aerosol face spray of water
- Blusher
- Petroleum jelly for your lips, or lip gloss
- Lipstick
- Lip pencil
- Eye pencil
- Eyeshadow
- Mascara
- Loose powder (baby powder will freshen makeup during the day)
- A sponge to even out makeup
- Soap and water or cleansing cream if you want to remove makeup entirely and reapply it

- A small jar of oil for eye makeup removal
- Skin toner
- Bobby pins
- Hair ornaments
- Hair brushes
- Combs   ,
- Brushes for liner
- Brushes for shadow
- Lip brushes
- Cotton swabs
- Cotton balls
- Compact dryer
- Eyedrops
- Perfume (use a scent no matter where you work, mill or office)
- Mirror

Some women keep aids that will help them to make a transition from daytime to evening looks so they can go out straight from the office. This could include anything from evening sandals to jewelry. For makeup, it isn't necessary to start over at day's end, but it will make you look better and actually feel more refreshed if you do. If you want to build on what you have, use a damp sponge to even out your remaining makeup and then blot completely. The blotting will absorb the excess oil or any grime.

Face color is important: Brighter cheeks will make you look healthier as evening light tends to wash out color. Lip gloss will bring sparkle to your lips, a light blue pencil on the inner rim of your eyes, and an extra-thick coat of mascara, and *voilà*, you're ready for the evening.

A last word about makeup retouching: In forties movies there are many scenes of successful businesswomen repairing makeup at tables of expensive restaurants. It is a *no-no*. Never repair makeup in public; and putting on makeup when other people are eating is awkward and rude. No one likes hair or perfume mixed with their appetizer. It's especially detrimental when you're trying to land a big deal during a business lunch.

Working Hair

According to a questionnaire which was sent to several hundred personnel directors before this book was begun, hair is one of the most cited beauty problems for all working women.

The major concern of thousands of women queried was the quality of their hair. The color, cut, texture, and length never seemed ideal enough. And women wanted to know what could be done about it. It's impossible to have strong, lustrous, "bouncy" hair without general good health and some external care and tending of your growing tresses.

HAIR HELP

To have good, strong, healthy, lustrous hair requires a five-part program:

- *Good diet*, emphasizing foods for hair strength, luster, and growth.
- *General exercise* to aid blood circulation and good, overall internal environment.
- *Scalp stimulation*, or a lack of nutrient-blocking stress and tension.
- *Brushing* that distributes the oils of the glands throughout the hair.
- *Hair conditioners*—a particular necessity for you who dye, bleach, or tease your hair.

Think of your scalp as a garden; your hair as its plants. Thus, your scalp needs to be cultivated and nourished. Cultivation includes exercise, brushing, and cleansing; and nourishment that comes both from inside and out.

Massage is the basic exercise for the scalp. Massage will increase circulation, strengthen the muscles, help normalize glandular activity, soothe the nerves, and help loosen the scalp, which, due to stress or tension, can adhere too tightly to the cranium and inhibit activity of blood and glands.

You can massage your scalp when sitting at your desk, at red lights when driving to or from work, or at odd moments. Use your fingertips only, or fingers and palms of the hands, and firmly but gently *move* the scalp. If your hair is in good condition, one minute daily should be sufficient.

If your objective is to grow hair, spend one minute morning and after lunch exercising the scalp with the fingertips; more if you feel tired or tense. It really soothes and relaxes. Some women have found that it relieves tension headaches, as well as relaxes the muscles of their shoulders since these muscles are worked when they reach up to massage the scalp.

A BASIC MASSAGE

- To stimulate the scalp, place the fingertips of both hands at the nape of the neck, behind the ear, and work the fingers up in tiny "steps" to the crown.
- Shift the fingertips to the hairline in front of the ears. Move the scalp around with the fingertips, and work the fingers up to the crown.
- Shift the fingertips to the back of the head to the hairline at the center of the neck. Stimulate scalp in upward "steps."
- Cover all areas of the back of the head.
- Return fingertips to front of ear position and work upward toward center of forehead.
- Place fingers at hairline at the center forehead and work fingers back toward the crown.
- Cover hairline from front of ears, working backward to the crown.
- Now pull your hair gently in small bunches to lift the scalp, stimulate the circulation, and generally encourage hair growth and vigor.

TO IMPROVE THE CONDITION OF YOUR HAIR

Find an empty office for this one, or save it for home.

Lie on the floor with your back firmly against the floor, arms at sides, palms up. Breathe in deeply; feel diaphragm expand while mentally envisioning the oxygen circulating in your chest and shoulders and up through your head to your scalp. Holding your breath, count to 10. Exhale slowly through your nostrils. Relax. Repeat three times.

While at your work station or desk:

Keep your face forward and, without raising your shoulder, try to rest your right ear on your right shoulder. Repeat for a total of 6 "ear rests."

HAIR BRUSHING TO STIMULATE SCALP AND HAIR

Choose a natural bristle brush that feels comfortable in your hand and is firmly bristled. Use the same pattern for brushing your hair as for scalp massage, starting in the back and brushing up to the crown. You can accelerate the benefits of increased blood flow by bending your head down to near chest level while you brush. The 100 strokes traditional in our grandmothers' or great-grandmothers' time is impractical and may not really be good for your hair. The objective is to brush all your hair, and how long it takes you to cover your scalp will depend upon the length and thickness of your hair. Brush with smooth, even strokes. Avoid short, choppy strokes. The slow, easy strokes are best for your hair and scalp and most relaxing for you. If you have long hair hold the hair midway to the ends to avoid excessive pulling and breaking.

THE SHAMPOO

Hair picks up dust and other debris from the atmosphere, as well as wastes exuded by the pores. A biweekly shampoo is essential, and washing your hair more often will not hurt it. If the atmosphere is polluted, you can shampoo every day. If your scalp sweats—from the atmosphere, heavy work, active sports, illness —shampoo your hair as soon as possible afterwards.

When you swim in the ocean or in a chlorinated pool and get your hair wet, rinse your hair with water as soon as possible to rid it of salt from the sea or chlorine from the pool. Both contribute to dry hair and scalp.

Before shampooing, the hair should be combed with a fairly wide-toothed comb so that it is free of tangles. (A tortoiseshell comb or other natural comb is better than plastic.) Then brush your hair thoroughly. Between combing and brushing, you might massage your scalp, but that's not so necessary if you are massaging daily. Choose your shampoo according to the condition of your hair and scalp. With the advent of the health-conscious, natural-products philosophy, many fine shampoos containing only products from natural sources have come on the market. Many contain herbs beneficial to hair health. Some are supplemented with vitamins, most notably vitamin E. The big commercial companies, sensitive to the public mood, are now advertising "herbal" and "low-detergent" shampoos. Read the labels, make your choice to suit your needs, and be sure the shampoo you choose has an acid pH balance.

Country rain water (not the highly polluted variety of water you might trap in the city) or distilled water is the best water of all for hair, but, for most, this is hard to come by. Most of us simply settle for what comes out of the tap. And this should be warm, and the final rinse should be with cooler-than-wash water. The cool water strengthens the hair by closing the pores in the shaft.

Many like to wash their hair under the shower, but some hair authorities think this is too vigorous for the hair, and not cleansing enough for the scalp. Some women like to wash hair in the bathtub, but it is difficult to rinse your hair adequately.

For most, the bathroom or kitchen washbowl is the best choice.

How to Give Yourself the Best Shampoo

1. Fill the bowl with warm water.
2. Wet your hair thoroughly.
3. Pour shampoo mixture into the palm of one hand or directly onto the head.
4. Work it quickly into a lather, using the cushions of the fingers. Work upward from the hairline to the crown. Work around your ears, temples, and the nape of your neck.
5. Rinse well.
6. Repeat the steps. (Two soapings is normally adequate unless you have dandruff, excessive oil, or have been in a particularly dirty atmosphere.)
7. Rinse your hair and scalp with fresh water a minimum of five to ten times. It's as important to free your scalp and hair from shampoo as it is to free your skin from soap. (You might do the rinsing portion of the shampoo under the shower.)
8. Make your final rinse with cool water—to close the pores—and lemon juice or apple cider vinegar—to ensure the desired acid balance of hair and scalp. Suggested ratio: one tablespoon vinegar or lemon juice to one quart of water.

Lightly towel-dry your hair. The first step in setting is to free the hair of tangles. Remembering that the water has reduced the tensile strength by about 7 percent, comb gently. Comb from the bottom to the top with a very wide-toothed natural comb to disentangle the hair more readily.

When you have your hair carefully combed, set it with pins or rollers. Use a setting lotion if your hair needs body and bulk, or if your hair style demands an extra-firm setting.

If you have time, it's best to air-dry your hair. Or if you use a dryer, try, time permitting, to restrict the heat to no more than medium heat. High heat dries scalp and hair. After your hair is dry, carefully comb it out or brush it, or combine brushing and combing, as you prefer.

HEALTHY HAIR

As your hair becomes glossy and full of body, you are likely to find that you want to style your hair with increasing simplicity, thereby putting the focus on the beauty of the hair itself rather than on the coiffure.

Nourishment for Your Hair

Since your hair is 97 percent protein, the first nutrient it needs is protein—in the diet and applied topically, too.

Protein conditioners are now commercially available for home use, and every beauty salon carries them and recommends them routinely as a post-shampoo necessity, before drying or setting the hair.

Panthenol is a miracle hair aid of the last ten years that is absorbed into the cells of the hair, where it forms pantothenic acid, an ingredient vital to healthy hair. Pantothenic acid moisturizes from within to help correct split ends, dryness, and brittleness, and to impart luster and pliability. Healing of the overlapping cells of the hair shaft can actually be seen under the microscope.

HOW TO USE HAIR GROOMING AIDS

If you buy conditioners, creams, or brilliantines to "control" your hair, read the label and avoid those that contain alcohol, which tends to dry the scalp.

Hair sprays should be used with caution if at all, or only on special occasions when the weather is humid or you desire a fanciful coiffure with no hair out of place. Most hair sprays coat and dull the hair. Some actually "varnish" the hair and scalp, closing the pores, a particular danger since the scalp—as other parts of the skin—is an organ of elimination. Some heavy sprays can actually seal pores, preventing normal functioning of the sebaceous glands. The result can be impacted pores and retarded hair growth, itchy scalp, scaling scalp, and even cysts.

HAIR PROBLEMS, AND HOW TO DEAL WITH THEM

If your hair is the victim of special problems, here is how to solve them:

Dry Spots:

If your scalp has dry spots, the night before you have a shampoo work a little castor, olive, or avocado oil into your scalp.

Brittle Hair:

To revitalize dry, brittle hair resulting from dietary deficiencies, dyeing, bleaching, permanent waves, over-conditioning, or too much sun and water, give yourself a hot oil shampoo.

Here's how:

1. Comb and brush your hair.
2. Part it in 1-inch sections. Twist up the hair and pin it so that it will stay in place.
3. Saturate cotton balls with your preferred oil and apply all over your scalp.
4. Massage the oil into your scalp well, so it penetrates into the deeper tissues.
5. Steam for 5 minutes by pulling a large plastic bag over your oil-soaked hair, a hot wet towel over that, and a dry towel or large shower cap over that.
6. Leave the oil on your scalp from 30 minutes to several hours.
7. Shampoo, using tepid water. Three or more soapings may be necessary.
8. Rinse with cool water mixed with lemon juice or vinegar.

Itchy Scalp:

Beat three eggs. Wet your hair with tepid-to-warm water. Wash your scalp with the eggs. Rinse with water plus vinegar and then with plain water. Repeat weekly for one month.

Dandruff:

There are many different types of dandruff, from dry to oily, all unattractive and all avoidable and curable.

Pityrasia capitas: In this common form of dandruff, the scalp is covered with dry, whitish-grayish scales or particles shed from the horny layer of the skin. If allowed to cling to the scalp, the particles cause itching. If the itching leads to scratching, the scalp can become infected. The condition can choke off the hair roots, and hair loss can be a consequence if the condition is not cleared up.

Regular shampoos, at least twice daily brushing, or daily scalp massage are musts. Applying witchhazel to the scalp also helps.

1. Part your hair in small sections and twist it up with pins as you would for a hot oil shampoo.
2. Saturate balls of cotton with witchhazel.
3. Rub the scalp all over with witchhazel.
4. Rub the scalp and hair well with a dry medium-weight terry towel to remove the scales.

Another topical application that has aided many is a sulfur and petroleum jelly treatment. Combine sixty grains of sulfur to an ounce of petroleum jelly and massage into the scalp nightly.

These homemade remedies can also be helpful in other forms of dandruff, such as *oily seborrhoea,* a condition common to young people and frequently associated with acne; and *waxy seborrhoea,* a condition where the scalp is covered by patches of soft yellow wax.

If dandruff is really troublesome, the first steps to take are restriction of starchy foods, except for whole grains and potatoes; reduction or elimination of milk and milk by-products; and elimination of salt.

Baldness:

Alopecia (baldness) comes from many causes, but it can be prevented and even remedied. *Alopecia senilis,* which begins in the mid-fifties and once was considered irreversible, is caused by the gradual slowing down of the regenerative processes of the body. It can be helped by vigorous massage and nourishment, from within and without.

Alopecia promatura. This form of baldness usually occurs

between the ages of twenty and thirty, but has been known to occur earlier and is generally attributed to heredity. But research indicates that important contributing factors can be a diet heavy with simple carbohydrates (candy, soft drinks, other sweets) and deficient in protein (fish, meat, poultry), vitamin and mineral foods (vegetables and fruits), and polyunsaturated fats.

Wearing tight hats and head bands is also considered a factor. Tight-drawn ponytails and African-style corn-row hairdresses which pull the hair tight are believed also to cause hair loss and balding, especially at the temples. The tight braids do not allow circulation in your scalp, and there is constant pressure and pulling on the scalp.

Alopecia areata: Also called "nervous baldness," this form of baldness often appears after an emotional trauma. Bald patches appear suddenly, ranging from the size of a pea to much larger bare spots. Alopecia areata is thought to result from a nerve injury or a glandular deficiency. Dermatologists frequently are called upon to treat this problem. The most widely used medical therapy is cortisone, taken in tablet form, by injection into the scalp, or applied as a cream. And sometimes tranquilizers are prescribed.

But before such drastic measures are undertaken, you should review your diet.

Foods That Improve Your Hair

If your hair is not strong, thick, and lustrous, and if you are worrying about hair loss, brittleness, and weakness, you should avoid candies, ice creams, pies and cakes, spicy and fried foods, and soft drinks.

Foods that are good for your hair are those rich in vitamins B and A and nucleic acids; such foods are:

- Fish, including salmon, sardines, herring, other salt- and fresh-water fish.
- Beef liver and other organ meats.
- Chicken, turkey, game.
- Fresh-cooked or raw vegetables,* including juices.
- Fresh fruits, including natural, fresh-squeezed juices.

*Particularly asparagus, avocados, beets, cauliflower, spinach, celery, onions, sweet potatoes, carrots, scallions, garlic, radishes, watercress, parsley, and legumes (lentils, peas, lima beans, soybeans).

- Eggs, preferably fertile. Eggs are best for the hair when taken raw, mixed into an eggnog in a blender with milk and a favorite fruit— banana, strawberries, peaches, etc. Favorite seeds, such as pumpkin, sesame, and sunflower, can be added, plus a tablespoon of oil. A tablespoon of oil taken daily on a fresh green salad has cleared up dry spots on the scalp.
- Cottage cheese.
- Whole grains—oatmeal, brown rice, buckwheat, millet, rye.
- Polyunsaturated oils, such as sesame, safflower, corn, peanut, and avocado oils.
- Monosaturated oils—olive and walnut.
- Wheat germ.
- Brewer's yeast.
- Kefir milk.
- Kefir yeast, processed from cottage cheese, agreeable to taste and offering the highest obtainable concentration of the B vitamins, a rating previously held by brewer's yeast.
- Water, 8 to 10 glasses daily, preferably between meals.

HAIRSTYLES FOR OFFICE WEAR

Today's hairstyles are elegant, sleek, sophisticated, and often close to the head. This look can be achieved with either short or long hair, and can be managed so it looks good both day and night.

Long hair: Your hair can be rolled up in a Victorian-style roll, with the hair tucked over "rats" or a net-covered base, allowing delicate tendrils to escape to avoid a too-severe look.

On some days, just allow your hair to float in soft waves. Shoulder-length hair looks wonderful this way, and unless you work near food or machinery, it's not a handicap. Loose hair is a glamorous style that makes you look relaxed and youthful. But it cannot be effective if your hair is at all dull or greasy looking.

The pageboy, a smooth style that is both sexy and classic, looks good on almost anyone of any age. Wrap damp hair around a roll of cotton, securing it with tape or hairpins. Keep the crown smooth and the hair will dry with just the right amount of movement and swing. Clip one side back for an interesting asymmetrical look.

Medium-length hair: If your hair just skims your shoulders, a full, rather loose look with heavy long bangs looks wonderful on youthful faces with good hair. It is easy to care for and is a perfect wash-and-wear style for every hair texture.

This next style is reminiscent of the fifties ponytail, but there is nothing "bobby-socks" about it. First brush and pull the hair back to the middle of the crown, and hide the covered elastic binding (not a rubber band, which damages hair) with a strand of your own hair, taken from the back of the bunch.

Short hair: The close-cropped head is back in fashion. Smooth and very neat, this look is not boyish, but very sophisticated. Brush your hair from the temple and ear on the right side of the head over to form curls on the top and left side of the face. Feature the one exposed ear with a dramatic earring.

HAIR CARE ACROSS THE UNITED STATES

Hair responds differently according to the geographic area in which you live. It can even be a weather report of the day's rain or dampness. The information below will show you how to cope, no matter where you live.

Northeast

Fall and winter days are hard on sun-dried hair, and the changes in climate make the hair flyaway and prone to static. If your hair is very dry and unmanageable, rub a small bit of cream dressing on your palms and work it through your hair. Don't cut down on the number of shampoos, but switch from an oily to a dry shampoo for a time.

If you notice an unusual amount of hair loss, don't panic—fall is the time for hair to thin. It is normal to lose between sixty and eighty hairs a day. With the approach of winter your hair will thin, but, happily, hair grows thicker with spring and summer weather.

Southeast

From Washington south to the Florida Keys, and west to Kentucky, the southeast can be a humid and difficult place for hair. To cope with humidity, try a strong setting lotion. In the summer, keep the hair covered and away from the sun as much as possible. This is especially true for tinted or colored hair. In the fall, a body-building conditioner can get your hair ready for the quick weather changes in the winter.

Midwest

The cold weather in the middle of the country makes hair brittle. If a Minnesota winter can freeze water and make your skin tingle, remember that it can damage your hair, too. The delicate oils and moisture in your hair strands are vulnerable. Chicago weather, with the strong winds and off-the-lake cold snaps, are disastrous for hair, and conditioners that are supplemented with oils should be used. Keep the hair covered at any temperature below 50° F., and keep it uncovered at any temperature above.

Southwest

Dry weather helps to hold a set but can be hard on the hair. Check to see that your shampoo and conditioner are suited to your local climate and that the mineral and alkaline content of the water in your region is not preventing you from having shiny, beautiful tresses. The open, relaxed, and informal lifestyle of the southwest is often coupled with a love of elaborate parties. Don't make the error of wearing an elaborate hairstyle during the day. It will make you look like a waitress in a 1940s diner.

West

In northern California and north through Oregon, rain and humidity make hairstyles go limp. Just as the climate can make tresses, grass, and even human skin lush and smooth, it can play havoc with your hairdo. Use a hairspray with an alcohol rather than a water base. And, use a hair dryer or a curling iron. Be very gentle with your hair. Damp and wet hair are more fragile than dry hair, so comb only with a wide-toothed comb, and hold your long hair with one hand while you brush or comb with the other to avoid pulling the hair.

Working Nails and Hands

Nails are much like hair. They are made of a very similar kind of protein called keratin. Like the hair, nails vary in texture, thickness, color, and strength. And, like the hair, you inherit the basic characteristics of your nails. Some people are born with strong, vigorously growing nails. Others have nail trouble almost from childhood.

The nail grows under the skin, behind the cuticle. Growth begins with a group of cells that are soft and gel-like. They remain soft until they grow out from under the cuticle into the air. It is the air that seems to harden them. As the cells grow, they keep pushing older cells out and it is in this way that your nails grow. The growth of the nail is continuous. It is always growing from the nail bed to the fingertip. You should be very careful never to harm the base of the nail where the delicate growing nail cells are formed. These cells are very sensitive and damage to them in the gel stage can cause the nail itself to be deformed. Often, for example, white spots can be created by damaging the nail bed.

Nails need the same care that skin and hair need: Cold weather and drying elements can make the skin on your face dry and flaky, and they can also make your nails brittle and prone to splitting. Water, soaps, and detergents can weaken nails as well. But the worst enemy of your nails is probably your nervous habits. Nail biting, flicking your nails, too much nail-tapping, and similar habits are very destructive to nails.

You can, however, encourage the growth of your nails by following these basic rules.

1. Never place your fingers or nails in any kind of chemical. These include solvents that can be found around offices and factories. White-out and error covers that are used in offices can be harmful to nails. Keep a pair of lightweight rubber gloves in your office. Make sure that you don't just dip your fingers into solvents and glues.

2. Get into finger-saving habits. Keep your hands away from any place that might be dangerous. Slamming and banging the fingers in drawers or doors and under lids can be very painful and can do permanent damage to your nails. Phoning or running any kind of mechanism that has a dial can be damaging to the nails, and though it is inconvenient, you can usually get into the habit of using the end of a pencil or pen or a telephone dialer to dial your calls. If you have buttons to press, use the eraser end of a pencil or your knuckle.

3. Never, never use your nails as tools to open envelopes, boxes, or knots. Use envelope openers or scissors. Be careful when you flip through piles of papers or reports. The biggest enemy of the nail is the stapler. Taking staples out of anything should be done with a staple remover. Be sure you have one in your desk or at your work station at all times. Use your fingertips, not nails, to pick up tiny particles, paper clips, etc. After coming in from the cold outdoors, when your hands and nails are especially vulnerable, press any elevator buttons with your knuckles, not your nails. If you are a typist, use the pads of your fingertips to type and use an electric typewriter, which is less hard on your nails than a manual. Also keep your nails short, as constantly banging on the ends of the nails can cause them to split.

Nails are easily gouged and damaged by scrapes and bruises caused by sharp instruments. Don't use metal manicure tools unless you are very careful. The cuticle is especially delicate. It protects the new nail as it is forming. The half-moon of white that is just above the cuticle is still in the gel-like stage before the final nail and is sensitive to heat, cold, and injury. Treat the cuticles with extreme care and always be very gentle.

Going without gloves in cold weather causes chapped hands and also dry, chipped nails. Even for just a few minutes, keep your hands in your pockets or in gloves. Be sure that you cover your fingers and nails with moisturizer every time you apply it to your hands and wrists, and that can never be too often.

The drying of the hands can be caused by the sun as well as the cold. Protect your hands and nails from drying sun, just as you would protect your hair or skin.

If your work is heavy, or if your job is on some sort of assembly line, wear gloves at all times to protect your hands and nails. The gloves will help to keep your hands safe from cuts and scrapes.

If you are wrapping, bagging, or folding paper products with your hands, try to use rubber gloves to shield them from paper cuts.

If you keep your hands in water or work with cleansers, detergents, waxes, rubber cement, glues, or solvents, always use rubber gloves as well.

If you find it hard to work with rubber gloves or any gloves on, tape each fingertip across the nail with tape. Use any type of tape that is available; the residue can be removed with just a wisk of nail-enamel remover, and your manicure and nails will last much longer.

If you think some dirt might get into your gloves during the workday, scrape your nails over a cake of soap to protect them. After the day's work, clean your hands and nails with a soapy sponge and a nail brush. Don't brush your nails too vigorously with a new stiff nail brush. Only the hardiest of nails can withstand that treatment.

If you are a schoolteacher or work with children or in sports, it is best to keep your nails fairly short by filing them neatly and evenly into a strong, rounded-square shape.

SOME NAIL ADVICE FOR ACTIVITIES OUTSIDE WORK

Keep nails polished and have an emery board with your sports equipment at all times. Some sports, such as golf, horseback riding, or cycling allow you to wear gloves to protect your hands. If you swim, remember that nails are porous and they soak up water. Never file your nails after a long bath or after swimming.

A GOOD DIET TO HELP STRENGTHEN NAILS

Your nails grow the full length of your fingertips in about six months. Injury to the nail bed will take many months to "grow out." As your nails grow, and for their general health, be sure to include two small servings of a protein-rich food in your daily diet. Eggs, meat, chicken, fish, cheese, and dried vegetables are all protein-rich. Strangely enough, many women report that their nails seem to become stronger when they are on a weight-reduction diet. Curious? Perhaps it is because many people actually eat better when they are dieting than at other times. They are more careful about eating the right foods, and they supplement their diet with vitamins.

FOUR SUPER HAND EXERCISES

1. *Finger weave:* Using a piece of wire or a pipe cleaner, try to weave the wire between your fingers, using only the finger.
2. *Chopsticks:* Use chopsticks often for eating. It is good exercise for your fingers, and you will eat more slowly and actually savor your food more thoroughly.
3. *Finger squeeze:* Squeeze a large soft sponge with your fingers. If your hands are stiff or sore, place the sponge under warm water and immerse your hands while you squeeze. Remember to cover your hands with a cream or oil before soaking your fingers in water for any length of time.
4. *Handshake:* Hold your hands at head level with the palms facing away from you. Shake your hands, relaxing the fingers and allowing the hands to flop over at the wrist. Repeat several times.

TIPS FOR KEEPING YOUR NAILS GLOSSY, SMOOTH, AND COLORED FOR MORE THAN A WEEK

If your nails tend to break and crack, you should consider protecting them with porcelain tips. You can get them through the mail from Annette Gordon, Ltd., 770 Madison Avenue, New York, NY 10021.

If your nails are stained with cigarette smoke or other discolorations, you can bleach the stains away by painting each nail with a coating of lemon juice. Use an old nail-polish brush or some other small brush and simply paint on the juice and allow it to dry.

If your nails are dry and rough, you can use ordinary vegetable oil to soften and nourish your nails. Wipe or paint your nails with cotton saturated with the oil, or paint the oil directly on the nail with a soft brush.

You can improve the circulation in the nail base and

through the pink part of the nail as well as the flesh beneath the nail by rubbing and buffing the nail with a chamois buffer or a soft toothbrush and tooth powder.

If you start your manicure with a base coat, and cover your nail enamel with a clear top coat, your polish will last longer.

Store your polish in a dark place—in a covered box, or inside a cabinet. This will keep the color true and the liquid smooth-flowing.

If your polish seem too thick, thin it by setting the bottom of the bottle in hot water.

If you want a thick, quick-drying polish, set the bottle in ice water or on an ice cube.

Polish your nails before going to bed. The longer you can keep your *freshly* polished nails away from water, the longer the manicure will last.

Every time you remove your polish, you will be stripping the nail's natural protective oil from the nail surface. It is better to repair small chips in your polish than to take it off and subject the nail to abuse.

When removing polish, do not scrub away the polish with a rubbing motion. Saturate the cotton ball with the polish remover and then hold the ball to the nail with a rubber-gloved hand. Hold the saturated cotton in place for the count of five. This will allow the solvent to melt away the polish. Then, with one or two whisks, the remainder of the polish will come cleanly away.

Cover newly cleaned or polished nails with softening oils.

Cover your nails with moisturizer or cream on a cold day. Your nails as well as your hands suffer from exposure in very cold weather.

CHOOSING THE RIGHT SHADE OF NAIL POLISH

Surprisingly, keeping polish on your nails can be good for your nails. Polishing your nails is often a deterrent to nail-biting and other destructive patterns, and keeps the nails strong at the same time as making them look better.

The shade of polish you use will change with the seasons and the fashion. However, a sensible way to select the nail polish color that's right for you is to coordinate it with the shade of clothes you are wearing, and the size and shape of your hands and nails.

The chart below shows some possible choices:

	Winter	Spring	Summer	Fall
black/white gray/red	red cherry scarlet	pink geranium fire engine	crimson vermillion cardinal	Persian red ruby chrome orange
brown/rust beige/cream	earthy tawny wine	coffee mocha bronze	cream beige golden-pink	mahogany sepia terra cotta
green/gold mocha/camel	apricot tangerine carrot	ginger burgundy maroon	toast pearl-topaz copper	marigold burnt ocher flame
mauve/wine mulberry/ purple	amethyst burgundy raisin	plum grape mulbery	titian coral mauve	pansy peach mallow
pink/violet lavender/ amethyst	cameo burnt rose orchid	lavender voilet lilac	tea rose primrose opalesce	cameo pink English pink salmon

HOW TO SHAPE AND COLOR
THE PRETTIEST NAILS FOR YOU

The shape of nail that is best for your particular hand depends on how long the nail is in comparison to your fingers. Your nail shape is usually similar to that of your hand. Long, slender hands with narrow fingers usually have long, narrow nails. Broad hands with short fingers often have wide nails that might be as broad across as they are long. The chart below indicates how to make the best choice for you.

Nail Shape	How to Shape	How to Polish
Square	Round off the tips, wear at a longer length to balance squareness. Do not color the square edges near the base.	Stay with light and medium shades. Get a more tapered look by leaving corners of nail base free of polish.

Nail Shape	How to Shape	How to Polish
Round	File tips into ovals, aim for a longer length. Color only the inner part of the nail.	Try subdued shades. Reduce nail width by leaving a bared arc at either side of nail.
Oval	File into ovals or rounded squares. Go to any lengths. Almond-shaped nails are thought by many to be most attractive.	Wear any color and paint the whole nail.
Narrow	Rounded-square (but not too square) is your best shape. Color to the very edges.	Avoid the very dark colors as these emphasize narrowness of nails. Color your entire nail.

TWO AVOCADO RECIPES FOR BEAUTIFUL HANDS

Using your hands at work calls attention to them . This is an old Mexican recipe which can be used on your fingertips and around the knuckles.

½ mashed meat of a medium-size avocado
½ cup of ordinary table salt

Mix together well.
Rub the mixture of salt and avocado pulp into fingertips and around knuckles and other trouble spots, like rough elbows. Use enough friction to feel the rubbing, but not enough to scratch the skin. The dead skin cells will sluff off in a miraculous way.

This next treatment for abused hands dates back to the early part of this century.

₄ tablespoons of sweet butter
mashed pulp of ½ of an avocado

Cream the butter and the avocado meat together using a fork or masher. The concoction should be oily and greenish. Apply this to your hands and fingers. Massage it in well around the knuckles. Your fingers will become quite slippery, so it is best to put on a pair of

Nail Shapes

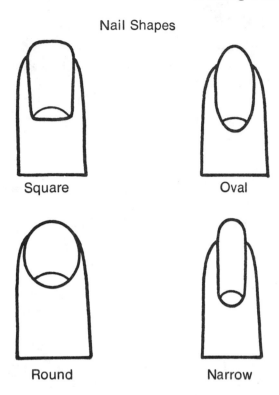

Square   Oval

Round   Narrow

plastic gloves over the oily fingers, or a pair of cotton gloves. Allow this treatment to remain on the fingers for about an hour, but longer is better. This will leave your hands soft, and the skin on your hands smooth and even-toned. And rough knuckles will be less noticeable.

YOUR DESK HAND AND NAIL KIT

Always keep a kit near your desk or work station with the following in it:

- A small container of moisturizer
- Several packets of towelettes to clean hands
- A small pair of cuticle scissors for trimming hangnails
- Small emery boards, to catch snagged nails
- Nail polish remover
- Cotton swabs and cotton balls
- Wooden orange sticks
- Color nail enamel
- Clear nail enamel

THE LANGUAGE OF HANDS

Your hands can be your most expensive beauty accessory on the job. A gesture with them can create a mood, or can be used to call attention to an object or area or to some part of your body.

Graceful movements create a feeling of calm and elegance; jerky, spastic, or disconnected movements indicate agitation and nervousness. Your hands are direct nonverbal communications. And the condition of your hands tells more about you than any fleeting expression on your face.

The most attractive hand gestures are natural and soft, without any violent or forceful sweeps of your arm or hand. Most women don't know what to do with their hands and fingers when they are in repose. This causes endless little movements that detract from poise and self-assurance.

Generally avoid movements where your hand is spread flat with the fingers either held together rigidly or spread like a duck-like paddle.

Hands look more graceful in profile than they do flat; semi-profile, with some of the palm or a small section of the back of the hand showing, is attractive, too. For a graceful view, your hand should be held sideways so that the inside of the little finger and the thumb are turned to be viewed.

Another graceful finger gesture is with the third and fourth fingers together and bent slightly toward the palm. The index finger and the little finger are less pointed.

Most of your hand gestures are instinctive. A jaunty or sporty mood will make you automatically hook your fingers at your hips or on your belt—a sporty gesture. A very feminine or delicate outfit will inspire a softer gesture.

Running your hands or fingers through your hair is a natural, very feminine, and expressive gesture. Any touching of the hair or face is thought by many psychologists to be an unconscious seductive gesture. Women frequently touch their faces as a natural reaction to many emotions. A hand to the mouth with the palm toward the lips indicates a mask of feeling; when the back of the hand is toward the lips the gesture might represent fear. The palm forms a guard in many situations.

Women in business should avoid touching their face or hair. Such gestures are not businesslike. And a masculine rubbing of the chin is even worse than a coquettish twisting of the locks.

There is another reason for not touching your face; it is because the skin of your face is very delicate and constant touching will enlarge the pores and stretch the skin away from the muscles. Constant touching will cause the skin to become slack and sagging. Wrinkles can be caused by constantly touching your face, or leaning with your hand on your cheek when you are thinking.

In our culture, the hand and hand signals are often more eloquent communicators than verbal or written language. From the wave, used for a long-distance greeting, to a firm handshake, hands are almost always in evidence. The following is a list of hand gestures that often can be spotted in work situations. You should be very aware of them, and listen to what they are saying.

- People who are in agreement often arrange themselves in the same or similar body and hand positions. Notice hands at meetings and discussions.
- Touching someone on the shoulder can have two opposite meanings—one to reassure, the other to restrain. Beware of anyone who clings to you.
- When the arms or hands are locked, it indicates that the person is resistant to the speaker. Watch hands when you are proposing a new idea or speaking with other workers.
- Horizontal gestures are used for emphasis. A hand gesture can take the place of raising your voice.
- Keeping your hands loose, relaxed, and the fingers naturally slightly bent indicates an open and relaxed attitude. Being relaxed and open makes others feel more relaxed, too.
- Gesturing to another part of the body—such as a hand to the heart or behind the ear—indicates a meaning that is associated with that organ; for example, a hand to the heart indicates sincerity, a hand over the eyes indicates that you don't want to "see" the point someone is making.

The beautiful actress Jennifer O'Neill has been quoted as saying that it is very important for her to be beautiful—right down to her fingertips.

On-the-Job Feet

Getting to and from your job has some special beauty problems. Wet feet, cold feet, cramped toes, or aching arches are painful, can ruin your expression, block your ability to concentrate, and spoil your day.

YOUR FEET

Your feet have a very sophisticated construction. They are made up of over two dozen bones. Seven bones are found in the ankle, heel, and back part of the instep, and five bones in the instep fit together to form the arch of the foot, a structure that is important in helping to distribute the body weight throughout the foot. Tendons and ligaments hold the bones in their arched position. When support of the bones is weak, the foot is flat, and calluses develop on the sole of your foot. The toes of the foot have fourteen different small bones that are similar to the bones in the fingers. In all there are 107 ligaments, 19 muscles, and 26 bones in your feet.

When your feet hurt, you hurt all over. The pain shows in the way you move and in tension lines on your face. Those lines, and the stiffness and discomfort of any movement, make you look older and certainly less attractive.

The state of your feet can encourage beauty or can combat it. It all depends on how your feet feel and how they move and function. All of that is dependent on how you treat and care for them.

The way you move, stand, and walk is a sure indication of your self-image. Walk behind someone, and just by their gait you can usually guess something about their personality and their general health.

Very few people even know how they look when they walk. Most people seldom see themselves in motion, and they don't realize how important their walking image is to their total look—and to their success. A graceful, natural, free gait is an asset, and anyone can have it with practice.

WALK IN BEAUTY

Just ask yourself how you walk and what can be done to improve it. Does your walk, for example, announce your age, or say, "I'm not worth it. Don't pay attention to me. I'm a nobody."

Are you a *timid walker*, one who walks with head down and bent slightly forward, glancing up only to look around? Her head might dart up momentarily, seeming to check the wind like a frightened animal. Her arms hardly move, she minces and probably clutches her papers, interoffice envelopes, or briefcase close to her side.

Or are you a *pompous walker*, hiding in a fearful, cynical, and defeated personality? This walk, with stomach pushed forward, is often favored by the overweight and is used to disguise feelings of inadequacy.

Then there's the *sexpot walk;* this gait is not unknown in offices. The steps are usually slow and calculated, and often it seems as if only the lower limbs and hips move.

The *sloucher*, on the other hand, is always overworked and tired-looking. The knees are usually held forward, the body relaxed, with the spine forming a letter C. Slouchers make others tired and depressed just looking at them.

The *skittler* scurries along the office corridor like a tiny little mouse. With mincing steps, neck forward, and nervous, darting little gestures and looks, the skittler zooms here and there, giving the impression of lots of activity. If only she would relax her shoulders, draw her head back, keep her chin up and level with the floor, she would look and feel better.(Note: People often ask the skittler to work late—with her mousy ways, she looks as if anyone can take advantage of her.)

The *pushy walker* marches along, not seeming to notice anyone or anything, thinking private and important thoughts and going directly for the target. She probably doesn't notice you—unless you're useful in some way. Shoulders move, arms swing.

and the stride seems long and purposeful. She marches to her own drum. This aggressive sort of walk is unpleasant and unflattering.

Get into the habit of checking yourself in a full-length mirror. Or check the length of your stride and the direction of your walk by selecting a path and noticing how many steps it takes to get to your destination. Then train your body to move with grace and rhythm, your legs swinging forward from your hip joints and not from your knees; your feet and legs preceding you as you walk. This will help you to keep your head back and your buttocks tucked under.

As you take each step, touch your heels to the ground first. Then the weight of your body should come to rest and be distributed along the outside of the feet. When the ball of the foot does come down, it should be in one very quick action.

Move your arms in the opposite direction to your legs: right arm with left leg, and left arm with right leg. A correct step is the length of your own shoe, or a bit longer. A man who is over six feet tall should have a stride of about eighteen inches; a small woman with very small feet, about size 6 (six inches long), should have a stride of about ten inches.

Keep your movements as fluid, easy, and relaxed as possible. Check yourself and your posture often. A peek at your reflection in a store window can be shocking. To see yourself is not vanity, it is just good sense.

Listen to the sound of your own footsteps. How "heavy on your feet" are you? Do your shoes flop as you walk? Do they squeak? Do you hear a shuffling or scuffing sound, indicating you are not lifting your feet correctly, raising them from the ground and clearing obstacles? Do your feet make a heavy clop and clump sound, indicating anger and a repressed desire to grind your enemies into the ground? If you walk in any of these manners, practice the following correct way to walk:

Keep toes straight ahead; knees close together. Let your legs precede you. Stand up straight with your shoulders back; your chin should be firmly level to the ground. Keep your muscles taut, and breathe deeply but naturally. Let your arms swing gently from your side, the palms of your hands facing your thighs, your hands and fingers relaxed.

It will be hard to remember everything at first, but like driving a car, playing the piano, or any active sport, there is a right way to do everything and in this case it is better for your health and vitality to work at learning how to walk the correct way.

Fourteen Ways to Walk to Youth and Beauty

1. When walking, look up, meet people's eyes, smile.
2. When walking by yourself, speak or sing to gain control of your breathing.
3. Be sure your walk and gestures are decisive; walk in a straight line, don't wander.
4. Stand and walk tall. Pull yourself to your full height by pretending your head is reaching to the stars.
5. Slouching, especially when you are tired or tense, only adds to the strain on your muscles. Count your steps, or play some other sort of walking game to take your mind off your fatigue.
6. Hold your muscles taut. Don't allow your potbelly to protrude or your shoulders to drop.
7. Walk in an animated, rhythmic manner.
8. Develop smooth motions. Avoid stiff, jerky, or exaggerated gestures.
9. Examine your feet every few days to be sure there are no breaks in the skin or tender spots. Every day, wash your feet and wear clean socks or hose.
10. Throw away any shoes that are uncomfortable. Study your shoes as you walk. They should not buckle or gap at the sides.
11. Wear graceful, high-heeled shoes. Pay more, and spend the hours needed to find the right pair of shoes with the right fit.
12. Be sure your pantyhose or socks fit exactly. Once you have found the right size, buy a dozen pairs—or at least two.
13. Try to change your shoes many times during the week.
14. Walk at least ten minutes each day.

Exercises to Help You Improve Your Walk

First, stand straight with legs and toes pointed directly ahead. Then lift your right leg and raise it to hip level. Next, swing your right leg around in an arc to the side. Point toe out to side. Move the leg from back to front. Repeat 5 times. Now repeat the entire exercise with the left leg.

Now try this one: Stand straight with legs and toes pointed directly ahead. Lift your right leg and raise it to hip level. Bring your leg, at hip level, in a circular arc to the side, and then as far back as possible. Note that your leg will probably have to be lowered as it moves to the back. Repeat this exercise 5 times with each leg.

Here's another: Stand straight with legs as far apart as possible. Keeping feet parallel, walk about 12 feet—the length of an ordinary room—with the legs held far apart.

Now collect about ten boxes the same size, line them up close together, empty side up. Grocery boxes work well. Lifting legs high, step from box to box. (You should not have more than one foot in any box at any time.)

This time, stand firmly on both feet. Move your weight to your right foot. Stand on the right foot only. Raise the left foot and swing the left leg forward. Bend the leg at the knee. Balance yourself with the right arm. Continue to raise alternate legs and balance with the opposite arms in a rhythmic manner. Practice this "pantomime march" to music while walking around the house (don't try this in the office!).

Or do these while waiting in line or in any office or home situation. *The Toe-Heel Walk:* Walk on your heels 5-10 steps. Now, walk on your toes for 5-10 steps. Repeat as desired.
A variation on this can be done even while standing on a street corner waiting for a bus, providing you are unobtrusive about it and don't care if anyone should notice and wonder what you're doing—and if you are wearing flat shoes: *The Toe-Heel Stand:* Raise up on your toes. Rock back on your heels. Repeat as desired.

Also try the *Newspaper Squeeze:* Put yesterday's newspaper down on the floor. Stand on the paper with your bare feet. Try to crumple each page of the paper with your toes.

Or do the *Ping-Pong-Ball Croquet:* Place a large plastic jar on its side on a large rug. Using six Ping-Pong balls, marbles, or even golf balls, see how fast you can get the balls into the jar, using only your toes.

Next try the *Book Bounce:* Stand on the edge of a phone book or other large book. Balance on only the balls of your feet. Let your heels down to the floor. Stretch your calf muscles and raise your heels to level with your toes. Hold for the count of 5, relax and repeat.

If you sit in high-heeled shoes all day, this is a relaxing exercise, the *Tendon Stretch:* Stand behind a chair, resting your hands on the back of the chair. Take off your shoes. Now move your left foot back as far as it will go, keeping your toes on the floor. Put weight on your right foot, bending the knee. Bounce back on your left heel. Change legs and repeat.

Ultimately, walking is the very best exercise for your feet—if you are wearing well-fitting shoes.

It used to be said that you'll have a healthy heart if you walk five miles a day. Now, in California, at the Longevity Research Institute, significant improvements in a variety of serious ailments have been reported with walking as the principal therapy, in combination with a special diet.

PERSONAL CARE FOR YOUR FEET

To ensure healthy feet, you must do everything possible to be sure they get proper circulation. This is especially important in older women when their arteries and veins are less elastic. If your feet seem cold all the time, or if your toes or toenails seem bluish in color, it is a sign that your circulation may be poor.

There are, however, certain things you can avoid which can add to the danger of slow circulation to your feet—pressure, cold, smoking, and infection. They are harmful because they make the opening in the vessels smaller so that less blood can flow to your feet.

Pressure comes from such things as tight shoes, stockings with elastic tops, and sitting cross-legged. Many doctors have expressed doubt even about support pantyhose. They are often too tight and constrict blood vessels in the entire leg.

Extreme cold should also be avoided whenever possible. Wading, swimming, or even bathing in cold water is really not good for your feet. If you work outdoors or travel in the cold, wear wool socks under your boots and take off your cold shoes or boots as soon as you come indoors.

A break in the skin, from which an infection can develop, is very dangerous. Prevent trouble, avoid any break in the skin—such as a blister, caused by an irritation like tight shoes, and ingrown toenails, or cuts from cutting your nails too closely.

When you have a few moments at home, put your feet in a tub of hot water—warmer than body temperature. Or use a hot water bottle or a heating pad on them. Use corn plasters to protect small injuries and irritated spots on your toes or other parts of your feet. Put medicine on corns to help dissolve them; but use the medicine only after carefully reading the directions on the bottle.

Do not cut calluses or corns with a razor blade or any other knife—there are special tools designed to "plane" or "shave" away the dead tissues that accumulate on the outside of the foot.

When you cut your toenails, do not dig into the side of the nail. Cut the toenails straight across and then gently file the rough edges. Very few people bother to file their toenails, but it is an important step, not only for the care and grooming of the toes, but also because it saves on hose.

While "self-help" with corns, bunions, calluses, and warts is common, certain practices definitely are to be avoided. Trimming corns with a razor is unsafe, even if you've sterilized the razor. Attempts to treat corns with acid corn removers aren't to be recommended either. But calluses on the heels and even on the ball of the foot usually can be eradicated by rubbing with a pumice stone. Castor oil applied topically can eliminate warts. If any problem persists, a podiatrist should be consulted.

Bunions often are a hereditary deformity, but ill-fitting shoes aggravate the condition. Bunions result from the big toe folding under the second toe. When there is pressure from shoes, the body responds by building a pad of tissue over the pressure point. Sometimes the problem can be alleviated by a splint or sling. If the problem is really severe, surgery may be the only answer.

Ingrown toenails are a common problem. To prevent them, the nails should be trimmed straight across—never rounded—and not cut too short. If you have ingrown toenails, the best treatment is to clean the corners and place a tiny wad of medicated cotton under the nail. Some people have reported curing ingrown toenails by opening a vitamin E capsule and applying to the infected area.

To avoid foot infections, here is a list of things you can do:

- Wash your feet every single day—twice a day if possible. Never wear any hose or foot covering more than once, and change your shoes as often as possible.
- Do not wear boots indoors for any length of time. If you work in an office, keep an extra pair of shoes in your desk. Take your boots off, and put your shoes on when you arrive at work. If you go to the movies or to someplace where you must wear your boots for hours, try to wear a thin pair of socks inside of the boots so that the socks can keep your feet at an even temperature.
- After bathing, do not fail to dry your feet carefully. And, of course, avoid walking barefoot in public places such as pools, swimming and health clubs, or locker rooms which might be breeding grounds for infection.
- As germ infections can take place when there is a break in your skin, inspect your feet at least once a week for cuts, scratches, tender spots, and cracks between the toes.
- If you have diabetes and you notice any loss of sensation in your feet or any unusual change in your feet—such as swelling or a change in color—or a change in the color or thickness of your toenails, report it to your doctor immediately

MOST IMPORTANT: WEAR SHOES THAT FIT

You may ask, "What are shoes that fit? What is a good fit?"

Well, first, there should be a minimum space of about three-fourths of an inch beyond the tip of the big toe, or your longest toe (if it is your second toe), and the shoe when you are standing with your full weight on the foot. The widest part of the shoe should exactly match the broadest part of your foot. The widest part of the foot is usually across the ball of the foot.

The shoe should follow the natural outline of your foot, and be snug but not tight. A shoe that is too loose is just as damaging as one that is too tight.

Here are the specific details of a snug, sure fit:

The shoe's *counter* should keep the foot in position.

The *heel* must give enough support. A heel height of about 1¼ inches for women is deemed best for walking, but there is no evidence that occasional wearing of very high heels has any effect on long-term foot or leg health.

The *toe box* ought to be round, high enough to allow space for the toes, and be of soft material. It should not press down on the toenail in any way.

The *sole* material must bend easily, be flexible and smooth, and keep the feet dry while protecting them from excessive shocks.

The *lining* should be smooth, with no ridges or wrinkles.

When buying shoes, be sure to try on both, as your feet are seldom the same size. The old cliché of "breaking in shoes" has no basis in fact; if shoes are not comfortable when you try them in the store, they will not be comfortable later. They cannot change their size and shape. Don't buy very thin-soled shoes. These are bad because they provide no cushion between the sole and the ground surface. Very hard soles are the same. Avoid wooden clogs, which are not good for your feet. The sole should flex, but the shank section should be firm.

Open-toed shoes are more comfortable than those with closed toes, not just for your toes, but because they allow more circulation around the foot and generally more movement.

When you change from a high heel to a flat heel, or vice-

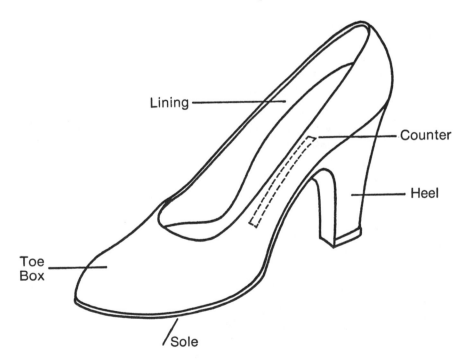

Lining

Counter

Heel

Toe Box

Sole

versa, do it gradually. Give your calf muscles time to stretch and rebound.

As shorter skirts and medium to low heels are making a fashion comeback, some books about career dressing advise a medium-heeled (2½″) pump for work. But many women find higher heels most fashionable and flattering.

Very high heels tend to jam the toes to the front. So you must be certain to buy shoes that are long enough and wide enough.

Be sure when buying shoes that your feet aren't cold. The foot shrinks just a bit, and your shoes will be too tight for hot-weather wear.

Shop for shoes at the end of the day. Your feet often expand during the day, especially when you are walking.

To prevent trouble, be sure to start wearing them for short periods of time. The best shoes are still made from natural products—leather and cloth. Each time you wear your new shoes, check your feet for redness, blisters, or sensitive spots.

HOW TO GIVE YOURSELF A PROFESSIONAL PEDICURE AT HOME

We've discussed how to keep your feet healthy with exercise, personal care, and appropriate shoes. But one of the most important details of beauty is the actual cosmetic grooming of your feet.

You should have a professional pedicure, or give yourself a professional-style pedicure, at least once a week. Plan to care for your feet during a relaxing time right after a bath. In that way, the skin of the feet is soft, and you are relaxed and in an unhurried mood.

You will need many of the same tools that you use for a manicure and a few extras:

- A flat bowl or basin that is large enough for your feet
- A little bath oil (optional)
- Several brushes (old toothbrushes, a nail brush, and perhaps a loofa)
- Hand or body lotion, or cuticle cream
- An orange stick
- A pumice stone, a planing device
- A toenail clipper or strong pair of manicure scissors
- A nail file or emery board

Find a comfortable spot for yourself and all your equipment. I keep everything in a small plastic bag.

Fill the basin with warm water and shake in a few drops of bath oil. Place your feet in the warm water, and relax, letting the water soak and soften the skin on your feet.

Gently wash your feet with the brushes, loofa, or a washcloth. Brush your toenails gently with the old toothbrush or nailbrush. Be sure that you wash between your toes, around the heel and the ankles. Soak your feet, washing and rinsing, for about fifteen minutes.

Rinse them in warm fresh running water. Then dry carefully, being sure that all the skin around and between the toes is completely dry.

Rub your entire foot, sole, heel, toes, and instep with hand or body lotion, and work the lotion well into your toes.

With the orange stick, push back the cuticles around your toenails, and clean away excess or loose skin. Keep slathering your toes with lotion as you work. If the toes seem gray or there is a lot of waste skin around the nails, clean the toes with cold cream and tissues, or soak the foot again, brushing away the excess skin with a soft brush.

Rub the soles of your feet with the pumice stone, and use the pumice on the edges of your heel so that there is no horny or hoof-like growth of dead skin.

If there is a large thick callus on the sole of your foot or edge of your heel, gently and carefully use a planing device to shave away the excess. Pumice and shave until the skin on the bottom of your foot seems soft to the touch.

Clip or cut your toenails straight across. Do not cut them too short. Allow between one-sixteenth and one-fourth of an inch of the white portion to show near the top, so the toe is protected.

File the clipped nail gently so that there are no snags.

Now you're ready for a final rub of moisturizer or body lotion, before slipping into your hose and your most comfortable pair of shoes for a graceful, healthful walk.

If your feet need a great deal of care, or if they have several corns and a build-up of calluses, you might want to give them an extra treatment at night. Two or three times a week, slather them with a rich cream and then cover them with socks, and allow the softening effects of the body cream to seep into the skin of your feet overnight.

Within a few weeks, your feet should be soft and delicate, yet strong, and delightful to touch and walk on. And yes—erotic to look at.

9

5

Working Nutrition and Vitality

Food for Working Beauty

In order to withstand the stresses of the work-a-day world, the working woman needs a good diet, one that is not only nutritionally sound, but one that keeps her at the weight required for her to look her best.

There is really no such thing as a "perfect" food, one single food that will provide everything your body needs. The simplest way to have a good diet is to have a varied diet, and to avoid the foods that provide only one kind of nutrient.

THE BASIC NUTRIENTS

If you want to be sure to include all the needed nutrients in your diet, here is a listing of foods that are the best sources of each.

Vitamin A—fish-liver oils, liver, butter, cream, whole milk, whole-milk cheese, egg yolk, dark green leafy vegetables, yellow vegetables, yellow fruits, fortified products.

Vitamin B_6—wheat germ, meat, liver, kidney, whole-grain cereals, soybeans, peanuts, corn.

Vitamin B_{12}—amply provided by small daily intakes of animal protein.

Vitamin C—citrus fruits, tomatoes, strawberries, cantaloupe, cabbage, broccoli, kale, potatoes.

Vitamin D—fish-liver oils, fortified milk, activated sterols, exposure to sunlight.

Vitamin E—plant tissues, wheat germ oil, vegetable oils (such as soybean, corn, and avocado), nuts, legumes.

Vitamin K—green leaves such as spinach and cabbage, cauliflower, and liver.

Folic acid—found in many foods. Liver, kidney, yeast, deep green leafy vegetables are highest sources.

Thiamine—pork, liver, and other organs, brewer's yeast, wheat germ, whole-grain cereals and breads, enriched cereals and breads, soybeans, peanuts and other legumes, milk.

Riboflavin—milk, powdered whey, liver, kidney, heart, meats, eggs, green leafy vegetables, dried yeast, enriched foods.

Niacin—lean meat, fish, poultry, liver, kidney, whole-grain and enriched cereals and brans, green vegetables, peanuts, brewer's yeast.

Biotin—liver, sweetbreads, yeast, eggs, legumes.

Pantothenic acid—almost universally present in plant and animal tissue. Liver, kidney, yeast, eggs, peanuts, whole-grain cereals, beef, tomatoes, broccoli, salmon.

Choline—egg yolk is best source. Liver, heart, sweetbreads, milk, meats, nuts, cereals, vegetables, soybeans.

Since your skin, nails, and hair are made up of more than 95 percent protein, the number one beauty nutrient to consider is protein. Complete protein is necessary for cell building and is available from fish, poultry, meat, milk and milk products, eggs, and soybeans. While Americans are known as "protein eaters," nevertheless many women who diet do not ingest adequate protein, and their wrinkled skin reveals it. The highly wrinkled skin of the very old is attributed by many in part to their inability to use protein.

Americans are also known as "carbohydrate eaters," because of their habit of eating over-sweetened foods. Carbohydrates are essential in the diet, but only the complex ones benefit the skin. Complex carbohydrates are found in whole grains, brown rice, fruit, a number of vegetables (including corn, lima beans, string beans), and some breads.

Americans are also prone to eat too much fat, consuming more per person than any other people on earth. Some studies set America's fat consumption at 60 percent of the daily diet. Fat is a dietary essential, but it is agreed that fat should constitute slightly less than one-third of your daily caloric intake for the sake of your skin, your hair, various body processes, and your general well-being. However, your skin and hair can't have sheen if fat is lacking in your diet.

Foods high in saturated fats are egg yolk, cream, whole milk, cream cheese, butter, solid shortening, coconut, coconut oil, organ meat, beef, veal, lamb, pork, and foods prepared with any of these products.

Foods high in polyunsaturated fat include vegetable, seed and fruit oils, fish, and margarines made with liquid vegetable oils. The polyunsaturates, along with lecithin, are credited with lowering blood cholesterol.

A good skin requires not merely a good diet but good assimilation, and assimilation can relate most specifically to exercise and including in our diet plenty of fresh raw and cooked vegetables, fruit, and adequate nucleic acids—the master molecule, deoxyribonucleic acid (DNA) and its "messenger," ribonucleic acid (RNA).

Nucleic acids work at the cell level, controlling production and functioning of the cells, the fundamental units of all living organisms. When the diet is well-supplied with nucleic acids, skin tone improves and wrinkles diminish and many other ills disappear.

The following chart shows the functions of vitamins and is organized as a guide to smooth and glowing skin and total beauty.

While vitamins have their individual purposes, they perform in tandem with other vitamins. Some cannot be assimilated at all unless one or more "partner" vitamins is present. Vitamins are needed to ensure perfectly functioning glands and tissues; when the balance is disturbed, cells deteriorate and aging is accelerated.

The best guide for nutrition is the U.S. government's recommended daily requirements. The chart below shows these requirements, with a special listing for pregnant women.

	Unit of Measure	Adults and Children More than 4 Years of Age	Pregnant or Lactating Women
Vitamin A	International Units	5,000	8,000
Vitamin D	"	400	400
Vitamin E	"	30	30
Vitamin C	Milligrams	60	60
Folic acid	"	0.4	0.8
Thiamine	"	1.5	1.7
Riboflavin	"	1.7	2.0
Niacin	"	20	20
Vitamin B_6	"	2.0	2.5
Vitamin B_{12}	Micrograms	6	8
Biotin	Milligrams	0.30	0.30
Pantothenic acid	"	10	10

Vitamin A (often called "the beauty vitamin")

Function: Helps keep skin and hair healthy. Builds and strengthens mucous membranes, particularly those around the eyes. Helps eyes adjust to dim light. Keeps lining of mouth, nose, throat, and digestive tract healthy and resistant to infection. Maintains tooth enamel. Vital to production of red and white blood cells. Believed to aid in delaying the aging process.

 Deficiency symptom: Enlarged and clogged pores; rough, horny skin on elbows, knees, buttocks, forearms; dry, coarse, lusterless hair; itchy scalp, dandruff, excessively falling hair; acne.

 Dietary sources: Beef and calf's liver, chicken and turkey liver, carrots, sweet potatoes, apricots, broccoli, parsley, spinach, watercress, endive, seaweed, fish-liver oil, cream, butter, egg yolk, bananas, and milk.

Vitamin B Complex

Vitamin B complex is essential to good skin, good nerves, good hair, good nails. Nearly twenty factors have been isolated. If dietary supplementation is felt necessary, most authorities recommend taking only the B complex, since most of the B vitamins work together, but some doctors have achieved what seems miracles with specific B vitamins for special conditions.

Vitamin B_1—Thiamine

Function: Aids nerve function, carbohydrate metabolism, good digestion. Helps body cells obtain energy from food.

 Deficiency symptoms: Depression, tension, insomnia, forgetfulness, numbness in extremities, swelling in ankles, lack of initiative, heart muscle degeneration, inflamed and fissured tongue, roughness of eyelids, sensitivity to light.

 Sources: Soy flour, beans, eggs, mushrooms, ham, beef, pork, lamb, turkey, bananas, kefir yeast, brewer's yeast, rice bran, wheat germ.

Vitamin B_2—Riboflavin

Function: Keeps skin around nose and mouth smooth, lip color healthy. Helps cells use oxygen to release energy from food.

 Deficiency symptoms: Pale split lips, inflamed and fissured tongue, rough eyelids, sensitivity to light, blurred vision, muscular weakness, burning feet, pimples, flushing of face, and waxy skin.

Sources: Milk, liver, kidney, heart, leafy vegetables, lean beef, veal, chicken, turkey, apricots, tomato, rice bran, eggs, strawberries, bananas, kefir yeast, brewer's yeast.

Vitamin B₃—Niacin

Occurs in all living cells. Forms part of the body's enzyme system. (Also known as niacinamide, nicotinic acid, or nicotin amide.)

Function: Helps maintain health of skin, tongue, digestive tract, and nervous system. Doctors prescribe niacin to prevent heart attacks, increase vigor and manage disorders of fat metabolism.

Deficiency symptoms: Rough skin, dermatitis, and diarrhea.

Sources: Liver, peanuts, fish, poultry, avocado, eggs, apricots, whole grains, wheat bran, yeast.

Vitamin B₆—Pyridoxine

Comprises a group of compounds, one of which is known to be active as a co-enzyme.

Function: Assists in assimilation of protein and fats; works with vitamins B_1, B_2, B_3, folic acid, biotin, C, E, and adrenalin. Believed good for hair texture.

Deficiency symptoms: In laboratory research caused skin and nerve lesions, anemia, cardiovascular ailments, fatty degeneration of the liver, kidney problems in animals on deficient diets.

Sources: Yeasts, beef and pork liver, salmon, herring, brown rice, bananas, pears, wheat polishings, peas, lentils, beans, peanuts.

Vitamin B₁₂—Cobalamin

Function: Vital to health of all body cells. Used in treatment of ulcers, psoriasis, shingles, rheumatic diseases, muscular dystrophy, hepatitis, asthma, osteo-arthritis, osteoporosis, migraine, and fatigue.

Deficiency symptoms: Pernicious anemia symptoms, including jerky gait, loss of balance, lack of coordination, swaying of body, inflamed tongue, fatigue, and emotional disorders.

Sources: Lamb and beef kidney, lamb, beef and pork liver,

beef brain, egg yolk, clams, sardines, oysters, crabs, salmon, herring, milk, and cheese.

Biotin

Function: Important to health of skin, hair, nerves, bone marrow, glands, including sex glands.

Deficiency symptoms: Most people can manufacture biotin in their own bodies, but antibiotics and sulfa drugs can destroy intestinal bacteria that produce biotin.

Sources: Yeasts, lamb and pork liver, whole grains, nuts, peanuts, legumes.

Folic Acid

Closely associated with vitamin B_{12} in function. If folic acid supplementation is taken while B_{12} is not present, irreversible nervous damage can ensue from pernicious anemia.

Function: Helps to bring blood into contact with all tissues and is used in the production of nucleic acid. Important in blood and hair health; used to combat hardening of the arteries.

Deficiency symptoms: Intestinal disorders, fatigue, pernicious anemia, depression, and nervousness. Baldness is believed by some to indicate folic acid deficiency.

Sources: Yeasts, dark green leafy vegetables, including spinach and beet greens; liver, kidney, asparagus, whole wheat, dried legumes.

Choline

Known to science since 1849, choline moved into nutritional picture in 1937.

Function: Patients with high cholesterol count can be benefitted by choline intake.

Deficiency symptoms: Laboratory animals died on a choline-deficiency diet; they also showed kidney damage. Anemia and heart and vascular disorders have been reported on a choline-deficient diet.

Sources: Lecithin is richest source. Good sources include liver, brains, kidney, eggs, wheat germ, soybeans, asparagus, Brussels sprouts, cabbage, carrots, peas, spinach, turnips, potatoes, and yeasts.

Inositol

Inositol was discovered in 1860 but was not recognized as a B vitamin for nearly a century.

Function: Some doctors believe it is important to slowing the aging processes, maintaining healthy hair and eyes, and for healthy skin and muscular tissue.

Deficiency symptoms: Retarded growth in laboratory animals.

Sources: Lecithin, heart, liver, wheat germ, oatmeal, molasses, grapefruit, oranges, peaches, peanuts, potatoes, spinach, tomatoes, and peas.

Pantothenic Acid

Converted in the body from panthenol, a pro-vitamin.

Function: Useful to combat signs of aging and stress; helps develop antibodies against infection. Panthenol creams are sometimes used after cosmetic surgery and skin grafting and to keep skin tissue soft and supple.

Deficiency symptoms: Eczema, nerve and muscle disturbances, heart trouble, susceptibility to infection, digestive malfunction, weakness, depression. Hair may be dry, brittle, have split ends.

Sources: Yeasts, liver, kidney, wheat germ, peas, soybeans, peanuts, brain, herring, fresh fruits, and vegetables. Easily destroyed in cooking.

Para-Amino-Benzoic Acid (PABA)

Function: Believed important for youthful-looking skin and healthy intestines. (Some believe PABA supplementation will maintain hair color and possibly even reverse grey hair to natural color. Hair color was restored in laboratory animals when PABA was added to diet.)

Deficiency symptoms: Deficiencies have been reported occurring in humans after administration of sulfanilamide, with resulting skin rash, fatigue, and anemia.

Sources: Liver, yeasts, wheat germ, meat, nuts, fresh fruits, and vegetables.

Vitamin B₁₅—Pangamic Acid—Pangamates

Water soluble.

Function: Increases available oxygen and is often prescribed in cases of heart trouble and cancer; believed to aid cellular health.

Deficiency symptoms: Not scientifically established.

Sources: Apricot pits, yeasts, rice bran, horse liver, steer blood.

Vitamin B₁₇ (Laetrile, Amygdalin)

First isolated in 1930 as a white, crystalline, slightly bittersweet, highly water-soluble, nontoxic substance later found to occur in the seeds of many fruits and plants.

Function: In highly controversial treatment, vitamin B₁₇ has been used to treat cancer.

Deficiency symptoms: Not scientifically established.

Sources: Apricot and peach kernels, cranberries, apples and apple seeds, sorghum cane sugar, filberts, watercress, alfalfa sprouts, mung bean sprouts, buckwheat flour, beans, seeds, nuts.

Vitamin C (Ascorbic Acid)

Vitamin C is sometimes called "the youth vitamin."

Function: Holds body cells together, strengthens walls of blood vessels, helps to heal wounds, builds bones and teeth. Important in manufacture of adrenal cortical hormones and collagen for the skin; important in forming white blood cells to fight infection; detoxifies drugs and environmental poisons in the system; fights stress; protects circulatory system from fat deposits; aids absorption of iron.

Deficiency symptoms: Tooth decay, bleeding gums, aching joints, tendency to bruise easily, susceptibility to infection, slow healing of wounds.

Sources: Brussels sprouts, broccoli, cantaloupe, citrus fruits, cabbage, peppers, avocados, tomatoes, kale, cauliflower, parsley, watercress. Vitamin C is vulnerable to the presence of air. Cooking destroys the vitamin.

Vitamin D

Vitamin D, "the sunshine vitamin," is fat soluble.

Function: Helps body use calcium and phosphorus to build strong bones and teeth; important during pregnancy and lactation. Vital to health of skin, bones, and eyes. When it is lacking, energy flags.

Deficiency symptoms: Poor bone growth, nervous irritability.

Source: Fish-liver oil is best dietary source. Egg yolks and fish are also sources. Sunlight produces it from cholesterol in the skin.

Vitamin E

Vitamin E, sometimes called the "anti-aging vitamin," is also fat soluble. It is chemically defined as alpha tocopherol.

Function: Used directly on skin to combat tiny lines, treat acne, and hasten healing after burns and surgery. Promotes normal growth, normal functioning of muscle, vascular, and nerve cells, acts as detoxifying agent, fights stress, aids absorption of unsaturated fats. Has been prescribed to treat infertility, as well as menopausal and menstrual disorders.

Deficiency symptoms: Skin disorders, anemia, gall bladder disorders, diarrhea, liver diseases, muscle weakness, nervous disorders, degeneration of reproductive tissue.

Source: Wheat germ, cold-pressed vegetable oils, especially sunflower and safflower, yeasts, cabbage, asparagus, and spinach.

Vitamin F

Function: Necessary for healthy skin, hair, and glands; contains lecithin, which helps sheath nerves, insulate and nourish them. It is believed useful in the treatment of psoriasis.

Deficiency symptoms: Not scientifically established, although lack is believed involved in skin disorders.

Sources: Soybean oil and flour, sunflower and safflower seed oil, peanut and corn oil, cottonseed oil, soybean sprouts, dried soybeans, egg yolk, liver, and brains.

Vitamin K

Function: Vitamin K is believed important to skin health. It is a blood-clotting agent.

 Deficiency symptoms: Bruising easily and failure of blood to coagulate.

 Sources: Green plants, including spinach and alfalfa; cauliflower, cabbage, carrot tops, kale, soybeans, seaweed, green tea.

Vitamin P (Citrin)

First extracted in 1926 from paprika by Dr. Albert Szent-Gyorgyi, who, in 1938, was awarded the Nobel Prize for discovering vitamin C.

 Function: Strengthens walls of capillaries; protects vitamin C from being destroyed in the body by oxidation; beneficial in treatment of hypertension and in building resistance to infections and colds.

 Deficiency symptoms: Capillary fragility: purplish spots on the skin, hemorrhaging. When vitamin P is lacking, the walls of blood vessels become porous.

 Sources: Peels and pulp of citrus fruits, particularly lemon. Citrus juice, paprika, green and red peppers, rose hips, black currants, and grapes. Citrin dissolves easily in water.

MINERAL MAGIC FOR STAMINA AND GLAMOUR

In the decade of the eighties, a better understanding of the role minerals play in the health of the body, the mind, the personality, the skin, and the aging process can be expected.

 Until recently, very little was known about minerals. Most of us seem to be adequately supplied, but there are scores of ways deficiency in a single mineral can cause disease. If your goal is vitality and beauty, you should consider a simple hair test made to determine *your own* mineral level.

 Hair tests, available from many laboratories, health centers, or health organizations, can determine your mineral and amino acid levels. Hair analysis is a tool in increasing use in toxicology. The tests work with dyed hair too. Simply send off an ounce of hair chopped near the nape of the neck. Hair cut from this area of the head as nearly as possible represents new hair growth.

A mineral lack can be reflected in depression, irritability, lack of energy and other problems, including dull hair and skin tone, premature wrinkles, and hair loss. A lack of minerals is sometimes confused with a reaction to stress and overwork.

The addition of one mineral-rich item to your daily diet can make a change. Try to eat fresh fruits and vegetables, fish and liver, and develop a fondness for such mineral-rich goodies as raisins, pumpkin seeds, sunflower seeds, sesame seeds, walnuts, and other nuts. There are successful, tireless women in their fifties and sixties who attribute their zest for living and nonstop schedule to a daily intake of pumpkin seeds, dried figs, dried apricots, raisins, or clabbered milk or kefir, and berries. These foods can be enjoyed in most work-food situations.

Minerals are needed in only minuscule amounts—"traces." Because these traces are so powerful and balance in the body is basic to health, it is simply not wise to supplement your diet without a doctor's help.

To be absorbed, minerals must be attached to a specific carrier, generally amino acids, the building blocks of protein. Minerals from foods, and in many supplements, must be chelated—coated with a carrier. Usually the carrier is a special protein in the body. A number of companies manufacturing minerals speed the process by chelating minerals, but not all manufacturing processes are alike. Do not take any mineral supplements without medical counsel or a hair test—except for a multipurpose mineral if you are drinking distilled water, from which, of course, all minerals are deleted.

Minerals can be miracle producers in improving health, zest for living, and lovely skin, sparkling eyes, and lustrous hair.

Here are some of the leaders among the nearly thirty minerals that have been identified as being important to health.

Calcium

Function: Regulates passage of fluids through cellular walls, to activate digestive juices, and to strengthen nerves. Calcium is needed for building and maintaining healthy bones and teeth. When your diet is calcium-rich, you are more vibrant, more youthful. Calcium must be in proper ratio to phosphorus—the body needs twice as much calcium as phosphorus. When there is an excess of phosphorus, a bond is formed with calcium and both are excreted in the urine. Vitamin D helps the body use calcium.

Deficiency symptoms: Porous bones, poor teeth, and poor gums, the most common cause of tooth loss. A study produced the finding that a calcium deficit of only 50 mg. a day will reduce the total mass of your skeleton by as much as 20 percent in a decade. Long-term calcium deficit is responsible for the fragile look of some older women. If you're working, it is vital to keep your calcium level high.

Sources: Milk and milk products, including cheese and yogurt. Apricots, kale, soybeans, beet tops, mustard greens, green beans.

Chlorine

"The body's internal scrub brush."

Function: Cleans toxic wastes from the system and stimulates the liver and production of hydrochloric acid, the enzyme required to digest proteins and other foods, including fiber foods. With age, hydrochloric acid production diminishes, and it becomes difficult to digest animal proteins. Chlorine helps maintain youthful agility and grace and aids distribution of hormones of the endocrine glands.

Deficiency symptoms: Hair and tooth loss, impaired muscle function, impaired digestion.

Sources: Kelp, leafy greens, ripe olives, rye flour, dulse and other sea vegetables.

Chromium

Function: Helps the body utilize carbohydrates; important in liver synthesis of fatty acids and cholesterol.

Deficiency symptoms: Some believe diabetes may be linked to chromium deficiency.

Sources: Polyunsaturated fats, meats, whole grains, and yeast.

Copper

Function: Required for iron to be converted into hemoglobin, the red substance in the blood cells.

Deficiency symptoms: Skin sores, lameness, general weakness, impaired respiration.

Sources: Almonds, dried beans, dried peas, whole wheat, prunes, liver, egg yolks, shrimp.

Iodine

Vital to intelligence; required to utilize fat. The body contains about 25 mg. of iodine, two-thirds of it being in the thyroid gland, and the other one-third in blood and tissues. Can encourage acne.

Deficiency symptoms: Dry, readily breaking hair; nervousness, restlessness, irritability, slowed mental capability.

Sources: Kelp, seafoods, all foods grown in iodine-rich soil. Onions are a good source.

Iron

Function: Supplies life giving oxygen to the cells; required to form hemoglobin; influences protein assimilation. Calcium, copper, and other nutrients are required in order for iron to function. Women need more iron than men, but anemia is not as common as once thought.

Deficiency symptoms: Cracked lips, poor memory, skin pallor. Chronic, bone-weary fatigue. Rapid heartbeat during exertion, occasional swelling of the ankles, pale fingernails. Headache, dizziness, shortness of breath.

Sources: Meats, particularly organ meats, egg yolks, fish, poultry, green leafy vegetables, avocados, lima beans, plums, peanuts, peas, popcorn, cherries, sun-dried raisins, dates, blackstrap molasses, endive, dried apricots, prunes, prune juice, fish, sardines, wheat germ.

Lithium

Function: Helps raise potassium levels in the body; helps conserve iodine; is frequently used in treatment of mental illness.

Deficiency symptoms: Nervousness, irritability.

Sources: Drinking water, sea salt.

Magnesium

Function: Called the "universal controller," it affects the "control points" of the cells, and stimulates cell metabolism and cell growth. Closely related to calcium and phosphorus in function, magnesium plays an important role in the building of protein tissue.

Deficiency symptoms: Has been related to delayed and difficult labor in births, loss of appetite, diarrhea, apathy, irritability, confusion, hallucinations, fluttering eyelids, spasms, tremors, sweating, paleness, rapid heartbeat.

Sources: Green vegetables, including cucumbers, figs, lemons, cauliflower, eggplant, grapefruit, yellow corn, squash, almonds, endive, turnips, apples, celery, walnuts, vegetable and nut oils, avocados.

Manganese

Function: Important component of many enzymes. Important in muscle coordination and strength; aids bone growth; moderates personality and is important in formation of thyroxin, the hormone produced by the thyroid gland. Effective absorption requires presence of vitamin E and the B vitamins, particularly pantothenic acid and choline.

Deficiency symptoms: Inconclusively linked to diabetes, multiple sclerosis, partial paralysis of facial muscles, blurred vision, difficulty in speaking and swallowing.

Sources: Whole grains, egg yolks, sunflower seeds, leafy vegetables, wheat germ, bone meal, avocados.

Molybdenum

Function: Aids in carbohydrate metabolism, prevention of dental caries.

Deficiency symptoms: Studies have linked deficiency to sexual frigidity and cancer of the esophagus.

Sources: Whole grains, particularly buckwheat, beans, lentils, and liver.

Phosphorus

Function: Found in every body cell and required for brain function. Helps create lecithin, influences protein, carbohydrate and fat metabolism, helps neutralize excess blood acidity, is needed for hormone production, and is important to kidney function.

Deficiency symptoms: A deficiency may contribute to overweight or weight loss, nervous disorders, chronic fatigue, and mental sluggishness.

Sources: Seafood, meats, dairy products, and many vegetables; avocados are a high source.

Potassium

Function: Works with sodium to maintain a regular heart rhythm, encourages muscle function, maintains the body's electrolytic fluid balance. Essential to heart function and nerves. Joins with phosphorus to send oxygen to the brain.

Deficiency symptoms: Heat stroke after intense exercise. Heavy sweating during hot weather encourages potassium depletion. "Relative deficiency" is considered common, especially during hot weather or after jogging or exercise.

Sources: Bananas, avocado, raw cabbage, turkey, chicken, watermelon, green leafy vegetables, tomatoes, beans, lentils, a variety of dried fruits, rhubarb, wheat germ, blackstrap molasses.

Selenium

Function: Believed to be very important in "de-aging" and "life extension." Has been used by some physicians in the treatment of cancer. Functions with vitamin E, and acts to protect vitamin E in the body. Only "trace" amounts are required.

Deficiency symptoms: No definitive studies have been made with human beings, but deficiencies have caused liver problems, muscle disease, and accumulation of water under the skin of poultry.

Sources: Foods from animal sources, including eggs, meat, poultry, seafoods; whole grain cereals, kidney, liver, milk, brewer's yeast, mushrooms, and fresh garlic.

Sodium

Function: A dietary essential required by the body as a conductor of electrical currents inside the nerve cells. It helps the body to maintain correct balance of water, and works with chlorine.

Deficiency symptoms: Excessive sweating leading to leg and abdominal cramps. Excessive sodium may encourage water retention, high blood pressure, ulcers, hardening of the arteries.

Sources: Muscle meats, chicken, eggs, fresh carrots, cabbage, strawberries, watermelon, pork, beef, lamb chops, squash, bouillon, oysters, peanuts, kelp, sea salt. (Ordinary table salt is a different mineral, sodium chloride.)

Sulfur

"The beauty mineral."

Function: Helps keep the skin smooth and youthful, the hair glossy, fingernails strong. Sulfur invigorates the bloodstream, making it more resistant to bacterial infections, auses the liver to secrete bile, works with B-complex vitamins to maintain healthy nerves. Used in protein metabolism and is part of the amino acids that build body tissue.

Deficiency symptoms: Dull dry hair, weak fingernails, "tired" skin.

Sources: Fish, eggs, lean beef, Brussels sprouts, cabbage, dried beans.

Zinc

Function: Considered essential for bone formation, necessary for mobilization of vitamin A stored in the liver; can aid in healing of wounds, ulcers, and skin lesions. Zinc is credited with clearing cases of acne.

Deficiency symptoms: Flaking skin, falling hair, short stature (dwarfism), chronic leg ulcers, delayed puberty, and slow healing wounds are products of low zinc levels.

Sources: Oysters, beef liver, lamb, beef, peanuts, wheat germ, seafood, eggs.

Every working woman should be concerned about adequate nutrients—vitamins and minerals—particularly during hot summer weather and severe winter cold spells if you work outdoors or spend long hours commuting to your job.

Stress can be caused by weather extremes and stress depletes vitamin C. Unless the diet is filled with mineral-rich foods, hot summer weather, which causes most people to sweat, can also be accompanied by a potassium deficiency.

Working women often suffer from depleted energy because of potassium deficiency. Potassium is a key nutrient, but the body only carries a small reserve of this mineral. Slow reflexes, weakness, and even clouded mental activity can be an effect of a lack of potassium. The body doesn't store potassium, but the stress of working seems to deplete it.

Good sources of potassium include:

	Milligrams
1 cup strawberries	270
1 cup gooseberries	233
1 medium tomato	244
1 cup watermelon	175
½ grapefruit	132
1 cup sliced cucumber	168
1 cup cooked fresh corn	272
1 cup diced, chopped chicken	575

Bananas as Stamina Aids

The banana can be a working woman's diet aid. Although somehow it has a false reputation of being fattening, it isn't. There are only 85 calories in a 6-inch banana.

The banana is a high-level carbohydrate, with very little fat and many minerals. If you try a banana with your coffee break or as part of your breakfast every morning, you'll notice an almost immediate change for the better in your stamina, morale, and patience, as well as an improvement in your digestive system since bananas contain pectin, a natural bowel stimulant.

Garlic, Sauerkraut, and Avocados for Health and Beauty

Garlic is also an important nutrient for women. In a Japanese factory where extremely high temperatures are maintained, whenever thirsty, one group drank ordinary water, a second group drank salted water, and a third group ate garlic pickled in soy sauce. Interviewing the subjects at the end of three days, it was found the women who ate garlic were much less tired after work than those who drank salted water or those who drank plain water.

Sauerkraut is also a wonder food. The bacilli of sauerkraut resemble those of yogurt. Sauerkraut also contains organic chlorine. Your body requires only about one-quarter ounce, but it must be replaced constantly for proper digestion. Sauerkraut juice at the beginning of a meal is an appetite stimulant, but sauerkraut in a meal produces bulk to help control appetite. A cup contains only 42 calories. So, eat the sauerkraut, but skip the roll and the frankfurter.

Avocados are nutrient dense. They offer eight essential vitamins, including A, C, and E; and five vital minerals, including potassium, magnesium, and phosphorous. Low in sodium, they have no cholesterol, and have complete protein—unlike other fruits. They are now available all year, and make a nutritious lunch food.

Your Diet and Beauty Profile

Answer the following questions and see what your working diet and beauty profile is.

Answer *YES* or *NO*

1. Are you within ten pounds of your ideal weight? _____
2. Do you feel satisfied with your figure? _____
3. Do you avoid crash diets? _____
4. Do you feel that you are as agile and active as possible? _____
5. Do you have a regular exercise program? _____
6. Do you swim, jog, jump or bicycle at least two hours a week? _____
7. If you smoke, have you tried to quit? _____
8. If you smoke, do you smoke less than a pack a day? _____
9. Do you try to get plenty of fresh air? _____
10. Is the area you live in pollution-free? _____

11. Do you drink mineral water or distilled water? _____
12. Do you drink at least 8 glasses of water each day? _____
13. Do you eat regular meals? _____
14. Do you include protein, vegetables, or fruit in every meal? _____
15. Do you avoid sugar and sugary foods? _____
16. Do you avoid salty foods? _____
17. Do you have a low-fat diet? _____
18. Do you eat raw foods? _____
19. Do you avoid "junk" foods? _____
20. Do you read labels so you are aware of the quality of the food you eat? _____

21. Do you take multivitamins? _____
22. Do you take mineral supplements? _____
23. Do you eat bran, brewer's yeast, or some other "health food"? _____
24. Do you avoid most alcoholic drinks? _____
25. Do you drink an alcoholic beverage every day? _____

26. Do you avoid tranquilizers or stronger drugs?   _____
27. Are your parents free from a serious degenerative disease,
     such as diabetes?   _____
28. Did either of your parents live to be over 75?   _____
29. Did any of your grandparents live to be over 80?   _____
30. Do any of your relatives seem very vigorous, though old?   _____

31. Do you get great satisfaction from your work?   _____
32. Do you enjoy what you are doing, most of the time?   _____
33. Do you have close and loving friends?   _____
34. Are you frequently nervous or tense with no reason?   _____
35. Would you be described as good-natured?   _____
36. Are you married?   _____
37. Are you secure in your job or work situation?   _____
38. Is there little stress in your work life?   _____
39. Have you developed methods of dealing with stress
     situations at work?   _____
40. Do you have a retirement program at your job, or are you
     planning for security in your program?   _____

41. Do you have health insurance?   _____
42. Do you visit the doctor for medical checkups at least every
     year?   _____
43. Do you take good care of your teeth?   _____
44. Would the loss of a job be devastating financially?   _____
45. Are you free of large debts?   _____
46. Are you seldom bored and depressed?   _____

If you have answered *yes* to over half of these questions, you should feel that you are well within a reasonable work- and lifestyle. This means a happier, and more beautiful, working woman.

FIGHTING FAT

Did you notice that the first five questions are about your figure, your diet, and your general body-image? Unfair as it is, you render yourself almost unemployable for most jobs if you are obese and difficult to employ if you are as much as twenty pounds overweight. There is a cruel prejudice against the obese. Women can be drunks, depraved, unstable, or vicious—and if they are slender they are forgiven. But, a loyal, ethical, and highly motivated fat woman can have a lot of trouble convincing others that they want her around. Most of this prejudice comes from within the interviewer, the supervisor, and the co-workers. In our society, fat means "loss of control." For most of us, losing five to ten pounds overnight would make us want to wake up in the morning! We would feel lithe, beautiful, full of energy, and happy.

Overweight plagues more than 50 percent of the women of America. Overweight may range from as little as five pounds to hundreds of pounds. Any overweight is a burden, and a dangerous one, producing many health hazards and obvious beauty problems.

To suggest that overweight is due to overeating is simplistic: Overeating may be the main reason for obesity but not the only one. Some people gain nothing on 3,000 calories a day. Some women gain weight on as little as 900 calories a day—or less!

Weight control requires a combined approach of dietary restriction and behavior modification, plus the *will to lose* and the *confidence* that the ideal weight can be achieved.

Not everyone should be thin. A five-foot-six inch woman may look and feel great at 139 pounds, while another of the same height can feel uncomfortable if her weight rises to 120 pounds. Bone structure is not even the deciding element in targeting an "ideal" weight; actual skeleton weights vary only a few pounds. In terms of diet, the primary need is to balance energy input (calories) with energy output (activity—mental as well as physical); calories alone are not the answer.

It is a recognized fact that many overweight women are malnourished. Gourmet, gourmand, or "ordinary" eater, the overweight woman can suffer from inadequate intake of quality proteins (meat, fish, poultry, eggs, milk, cheese, butter, soybeans), or "complex" carbohydrates, as represented by whole grains, brown rice, vegetables, and fruit, and vitamin- and mineral-rich foods—cooked and raw vegetables and fruit, primarily.

On a carefully selected diet, weight will stabilize, the overly thin gaining on a diet that will cause the overly fat to lose. The key to this miracle is to incorporate foods into the diet that help "spark" the metabolism, and encourage assimilation, utilization, and good elimination.

A woman who wants to lose weight is likely to feel virtuous eating steak, tomatoes, and lettuce, but she shouldn't. It isn't a balanced meal, and the calories of that steak would be better invested in low-calorie fish, such as salmon, and additional foods the body needs.

For instance, 3 ounces of beef steak represent from 350 to

415 calories; 16.2 grams protein; 38.2 grams fat; 8 mg. calcium; 139 mg. phosphorus; 2.1 mg. iron; 40 mg. sodium; 181 mg. potassium; 70 International Units of vitamin A; .05 mg. thiamin; .14 mg. riboflavin, and 3.4 mg. niacin, vs, for 3 ounces of salmon, 156 calories; 23.1 grams protein; 6.3 grams fat; 351 mg. phosphorus; .9 mg. iron; 99 mg. sodium; 378 mg. potassium, 150 International Units of vitamin A, 1.5 mg. thiamin; .06 mg. riboflavin, and 8.4 mg. niacin.

On a balanced diet of 1,000 calories a day, it is possible to have a first week weight loss as high as ten pounds. That ten-pound loss is probably primarily water. A more usual weight loss on a basic, balanced, restricted calories diet is one-half to one pound per week, which can mean that a person can lose over fifty pounds in a year. When such a loss is achieved slowly, there is good opportunity to have the skin reduce to fit the reduced body.

When calorie counting is made the basis for weight loss, it is *essential* that you make clear distinction between "good" and "bad" (or "empty") calories. When you consume 300 calories in a piece of the usual Danish pastry from a coffee shop, you gain virtually nothing but calories. If you ate the same number of calories in a cake made with walnuts, carrots, raisins, and honey, you would gain very real values with calories—vitamin A, phosphorus, calcium, potassium, thiamin, riboflavin, niacin, iron, sodium, and even a little vitamin C.

If you have a weight problem, you should consult a doctor. When you do, there are some facts he will need to know—facts only you can provide. Before you embark on a weight-reducing program, on your own or under medical supervision, for several days keep a running account of *everything* you eat and drink, not only the items but the sizes and weights of the portions (so you can estimate weight or calories), and keep a list of ingredients used for food you prepare, such as oil or butter or margarine for sautéing, oil in salad dressing, sugar, and so on.

A small notebook for recording the calorie count of common foods can be kept. Write to the U.S. Department of Agriculture for a calorie food list. And with this, estimate the number of calories you are taking in each day, counting them up for each meal and snack. If your servings are larger than the portions given, increase your calorie count accordingly.

If your weight has been stabilized at its present undesirable level for several months, you should be able to reduce at the rate of 1 to 2 pounds per week simply by eliminating 500 to 1,000 calories from your daily diet. If you are *currently gaining,* however, a reduction of 500 to 1,000 calories is not likely to produce a weekly weight loss of even one-half to one pound. You may need to cut your calorie intake even further.

Unless your doctor prohibits it, you should exercise one or more times a day when you diet, but your day should include a rest period too, and plenty of sleep at night.

Weight loss based on balanced low-calorie diets are traditional and are believed best by many obesity specialists, including Dr. Jerome Knittle, director of obesity research at New York's famed Mt. Sinai Hospital. Other doctors have also had extraordinary successes with high-protein, low-carbohydrate diets, and even no carbohydrate or no fat diets. But such diets require continuous medical supervision.

The simplest high-protein, low-carbohydrate diet requires only that you eliminate all sugars and starches. As long as you lose on this diet, no other change is required. If you reach a plateau and stay there for a week, but have not yet attained your ideal weight, then the recommendation is that you restrict your carbohydrate intake further. For example, reduce your fruit and vegetable intake to one or two a day, including juices, eliminate your intake of such carbohydrate vegetables as lima beans, and drastically reduce your intake of milk, including cottage cheese. On this diet, cream, including whipped cream, bacon, and ham are not restricted.

A diet of only high protein *should never be undertaken* except under medical guidance. Such a diet is not for women with high blood pressure, diabetes, kidney, liver, renal, thyroid, or heart problems, or other diseases. It is also contraindicated during pregnancy and nursing.

Fad Diets

This form of dieting is easier for many than the low-calorie diet, but should only be undertaken after a medical check-up and under a doctor's guidance.

If you are one who cannot handle a high-protein diet, and cannot or prefer not to go the "balanced diet–low calorie" route, a diet based on rice—preferably the most nutritious brown rice—will take the pounds off. Your diet, however, is not confined to rice alone. You eat vegetables and fruits, too, and milk products—skim or low-fat milk—cottage and other low-calorie cheeses and, if it suits you, a small amount of lean fish, poultry, and lean meat. This diet has been perfected in some university test centers, and works well for very obese women.

Choosing Foods for Your Diet

If you choose the low-calorie, balanced diet way to lose weight and keep it off, here are some basic points to remember:

Foods to Avoid: Cakes, pies, candy, ice cream, cream, french fried potatoes, pretzels, potato chips, cheese-flavored snacks and similar party snacks; sweetened yogurt, sweetened fruit drinks, sweetened canned fruit, pastries, pancakes, waffles, gravies, sauces of all kinds, doughnuts, hot dogs, hamburgers in a bun.

Foods to Eat with Caution: Macaroni, spaghetti, puddings, raisins and other dried fruits, most delicatessen foods, nuts, mayonnaise, cream cheese, hard cheese, condiments.

For example, restrict yourself to one-half cup of macaroni or spaghetti, no oftener than once a week; to one tablespoon chopped nuts; one teaspoon mayonnaise at a time or two teaspoons artificial mayonnaise; two tablespoons of chili sauce, one teaspoon butter, one teaspoon peanut butter, four teaspoons sour cream.

Foods to Eat with Extreme Caution: Honey, sugar, blackstrap or other molasses.

Foods to Eat Freely: Raw green vegetables, zucchini, celery, radishes, mushrooms, cucumbers, watercress, dandelions, grapefruit, plain gelatin.

Foods to Eat Daily: Milk or milk products, including buttermilk, cottage cheese, or plain yogurt, regular or low calorie.

Whole grain cereals, such as oatmeal, millet, buckwheat, and brown rice.

Whole grain bread—one slice a day, or two slices on a day when you do not eat a whole grain cereal.

Vegetables—raw and cooked, green and yellow, two or more servings daily.

Fruits—raw and/or cooked if desired, provided cooking is done without adding sugar, honey, or any kind of sweetened syrup.

Fats—butter, mayonnaise (regular) or oil or margarine, up

to one tablespoon represented by any one or a variety of fats. Sour cream can be counted within your fat allowance at a ratio of four teaspoons of sour cream versus one teaspoon of butter or peanut butter; catsup or chili sauce at a ratio of two tablespoons versus one teaspoon butter; nuts at a ratio of one tablespoon versus one teaspoon butter.

Additional Tips:

- Don't fry food.
- Trim visible fat from meat and cook on a rack so the fat will drain off.
- Don't tempt yourself by buying forbidden foods.
- Use fluid or dry skim milk, buttermilk, and soft cheese made from skim milk.
- Limit your use of hard cheese to not more than one serving per week.
- Don't add butter or sour cream to baked potatoes, fish, or fruits.
- Limit yourself to not more than two slices of bread daily.
- Take small servings—generally no more than one-half cup of any food.
- Eliminate seconds.
- Make a habit of leaving a small amount of food on your plate even though the portions are small. It will help you get over the "clean plate" habit.
- Eat slowly. This will encourage you to savor the food you eat, help you satisfy your hunger more easily, and will allow more time for your brain to direct your hand to stop the plate-to-mouth action.
- Make low-calorie snacks a habit so that you will eat less at mealtime.
- Avoid dishes that call for breading, crumbing, or flouring. (If you are accustomed to rolling chicken in flour or oil before roasting, try rubbing it inside and out with lemon juice, a slivered clove of garlic, and kosher salt.) Roast a 3½ lb. chicken in a 350°F. oven for 1 hour, and you will revel in its juicy tastefulness.
- If you are going to a meeting or a party where carbohydrates are inevitably served, take along your own care package filled with such goodies as raw carrots, zucchini, celery, cauliflower, and a small container filled with low-calorie yogurt as a dip. You won't be pitied. You'll be envied.
- Vary your diet so that you will be sure to get a full array of the essential nutrients.
- Two fresh fruits a day is a good rule for a woman; three, for a man.
- Ensure your vitamin A intake with liver once a week. But this and other organ meats should be avoided by anyone with a high uric-acid level.
- *See* yourself thin.
- Practice being happy!

Don't talk about your diet. It's safer. People who are fat will commiserate with you or may even say you look terrible, etc. And thin people rarely understand your problem.

Excess weight is a health burden; and there is more than one way to shed those excess pounds and keep them off. Choose the way that suits you best—physically and emotionally. It is actually possible to enjoy losing weight. Not only can you experience the joy of seeing the pounds drop off, but you can actually like your diet.

Dieting in Restaurants

While you are on your diet, you'll be eating out, so keep the following in mind:

Surprisingly, pizza restaurants are really wonderful for the nutrition-minded dieter. Order green peppers, onions, or tomato pizzas, but remember to leave about half the bread on the plate.

Chinese restaurants are wonderful for high protein and quick-cooked vegetables. Order a steamed fish, or if you just want a light snack, one egg roll and a small cup of clear soup, such as wonton (the wonton will add about 50 calories to the soup), with a small fruit dessert makes a perfect meal. No, you cannot have the fried noodles.

Mexican and Spanish restaurants are tempting because the rice and spices are so exciting. But pass them by, and only eat the fillings to the tacos. Chili con carne is probably the main reason for Elizabeth Taylor's figure; it is habit-forming.

French restaurants offer great variety: Omelettes, broiled meats, or fish, with a small order of boiled vegetables, are perfect. If you can, order all the food without sauce, and garnish with lemon juice.

Italian food includes fresh green salads, and wonderful shrimp and seafoods. A small order of pasta is not as calorie-laden as most people think.

American steakhouses serve huge steaks, and most foods are swimming in butter. Avoid any relishes, and eat only half the meat, after trimming away all the fat. Scrape off the butter, using your knife.

Drink a glass of cold water at meals. The cold water will desensitize your stomach and fill it. It's a great aid to cutting back on food. Keep a mental calculation of what you eat, adding each mouthful as you chew it; the process is so demoralizing and tedious that you'll stop eating after your initial hunger is satisfied.

No matter where you are, no matter what sort of main dish you order, you really cannot eat any of the following and expect to lose weight. So, say no to: butter, cream, sour cream, whole milk, most cheeses, salad dressings, sauces, creamed foods, thickeners, nondairy substitutes (they contain oils), shortening, lard, pork, poultry skin, bacon, sausage, frankfurters, luncheon meats, pate[1], biscuits, muffins, doughnuts, rolls, cakes, cookies, pies, cupcakes, baked goods, frozen or canned foods, prepared dinners, casseroles, dried fruits, grapes, cherries and watermelon, ice cream, milk sherbet, puddings, mousse, candies, nuts, chocolate, and beans.

Say yes to: fruits for dessert, herbs used instead of salt, broiled, baked or boiled meats and fish, trimmed meat and poultry, all meat served on toast (don't eat the toast; just let it soak up the oils from the meats), yogurt instead of mayonnaise, fresh vegetable garnishes rather than olives or nuts.

How to Order a Working Woman's Lunch:

Turn down cocktails; they often have sugar in them. A low-calorie drink, mineral water, or a small glass of wine is best.

Either skip the appetizers or order only an appetizer for your entire lunch. A good shrimp cocktail will cost you almost as much as a sandwich, and with only lemon juice on it, it will provide the needed protein for your entire day's requirements.

Order consommé, or a clear soup of any kind, if you enjoy it. Onion soup is fine, but any cheese or bread in the soup must be counted as an extra.

For your entrée, select broiled dishes, and never lose sight of the quantity you are eating. A hamburger about half the size of your palm and about as thick is 250 calories. And gravy, sauce, bread or fried foods are out. If you order liver, sweetbreads, or other organ meats, they will probably be fried or cooked with butter or some other sauce which adds calories.

Salads, greens, and vegetables can be just as forbidden as french fries if they are covered with dressings or mayonnaise. Vegetables contain no cholesterol and very little fat, so they are acceptable. A small entrée of cooked vegetables could be your main course, although it may not be as filling as some other dishes.

A medium-sized boiled potato has only about 85 calories. Jacqueline Onassis is supposed to dine on a baked potato (90 calories) and a half teaspoon of caviar (about 100 calories) to keep her perfect figure. But a serving of fried potatoes has 275 calories. So, it isn't the food, but the preparation that is important with many vegetables as well as salads and meats.

Breads, rolls, and muffins are dreadful, not just because they are breadstuffs, but because they invite butter. And good bread can actually stimulate appetite. If you really want bread, try dry whole wheat bread and pass up the sweet rolls or corn muffins which are twice as fattening.

Desserts, except for a fruit, or "Italian" ices which are mostly water, should be passed by. If you love something sweet with your coffee, ask about a mint candy, which has about 25 calories, fewer than a large bite of cheese cake.

A sandwich for lunch is splendid—if you don't eat the bread, and if the meat or filling is not covered with dressing. Don't feel shy about undressing your sandwich, piling the bread on the side of the dish, and attacking the filling with a knife and fork.

Watch out for the "low-calorie" entrée, or a slimming salad that many restaurants include on their menu. Most of those prepared plates have gobs of sugar-loaded gelatin and are not really low in calories at all. And cottage cheese, while lower in calories than many of the hard cheeses, will take up about 200 calories, unless it is made from low-fat skim milk. The usual plate of small salad, hamburger, and cottage cheese touted as high-protein-low-calorie can actually stack up to 500 calories.

When in doubt, a plain or herb omelette will probably be only 300 to 350 calories.

Avoid junk foods whenever possible as they are not only bad in themselves, but diminish a desire for foods that are good for you. And they add calories.

The "worst" junk food choices are:

• Cola-flavored drinks—not only because of their calories, but because of their caffeine. People can become cola-holics and really addicted to these drinks, consuming several bottles daily.
• Refined white flour. The wheat germ and the nutritious, outside layers of grain have been removed, and the chlorine dioxide used in bleaching the flour is considered a health hazard.

- Sweet rolls and others pastries made with refined white flour and sugar.
- Chocolate bars and chocolate candy.
- Commercial fruit drinks. These are primarily water and sugar containing only a fraction of real fruit juice, plus chemicals as preservatives. Some powdered fruit drinks actually contain no real fruit at all.
- Heavily salted snack foods.
- Potato chips.
- Commercial ice cream, which is often loaded heavily with chemicals.
- Imitation foods, such as egg and dairy substitutes and "instant" breakfasts, which represent only a fragment of the values of the real food even though sometimes the taste is maintained.
- Coffee.

FAST FOOD AND TAKE-OUT FOODS FOR OFFICE EATING

Because so many of us who eat out eat fast foods, and because precooked foods are so convenient for the working woman (and man), the U.S. government and several private consumer groups have attempted to provide nutritional guides. The following is a list of fast-food dishes and the protein content of some of them:

Fast Foods	% of Daily Protein Requirement
Chopped beef or hamburger	55-65
Roast beef sandwich	55-65
Pizza	55-70
Fish	60-72
Fried chicken	60-80

The amount of protein will vary with the serving size and the original produce. And, the amount of protein in a serving has very little to do with the number of calories in the serving.

With a little planning, and some care, you can enjoy fast-food snacks during work, or after work as a quick dinner.

The simplest way to make sure that you're getting the most from your fast foods is to be sure you get a nutritionally balanced daily diet. This can be done by being sure you get some of each of the basic foods every day.

Here is the way you can eat from machines, coffee carts,

hamburger spots, fast-food restaurants, delicatessens, take-out sections of supermarkets, and sidewalk vendor carts.

Breakfast: Most people eat breakfast at home, but then they enjoy a midmorning coffee break or snack at work. Buy a small bag of raisins, some nuts (unsalted), crackers that have high fiber, an apple, or even a piece of cheese. Pass by the Danish or sweet rolls.

Lunch: Sandwich choices include: low-calorie turkey or chicken white meat, sliced eggs, boiled ham rather than spiced ham, or other high-calorie luncheon meats, lean hamburgers (preferably without the roll), or a small container of cottage cheese (about 200 calories a container).

At supermarket take-outs, or delicatessens, order 3 ounces of meat or hard cheese at about 100 calories for each ounce or 1-inch cube.

Or buy clear, freshly made vegetable soup, without salt (there is sugar and salt in almost every canned, packaged food). Or buy yogurt, fruit juices (the unsugared kind), or small packets of nuts from vending machines.

Your office coffee-carts are also responding to interest in nutrition by carrying fresh fruit and small portions of cheese.

For it to work efficiently, your diet should be combined with exercise, although not necessarily a formal exercise program.

BALANCING YOUR CALORIES AND ACTIVITY

To calculate what your daily caloric intake should be, you need to take into account your build and activity pattern. A small-boned person of small stature requires far fewer calories than a heavy-boned, tall person. A very active person can afford to take in far more calories than a sedentary person.

Most adult females in office or service jobs rate as sedentary.

You are "sedentary" if you spend most of your time sitting, standing, and moving around in a relatively small space, and if your recreation is occasional and mild (such as swimming and dancing). Into this category fall the majority of professional and white collar workers, indoor blue collar workers, laboratory technicians, and clerical and creative workers.

In the "active" category are those who move fast and continuously, such as postal employees, sales clerks, gardeners, farmers, cleaning personnel, factory workers, and teachers. The "very active" category includes construction workers, waitresses, miners, loggers, and amateur and professional athletes or coaches.

To estimate your total *daily energy need*, multiply your desirable body weight by:

- 16 calories, if you are sedentary;
- 20 calories, if you active;
- 24 calories, if you are very active.

To lose weight, you must take in fewer calories than your total daily energy need so that body fat will be oxidized to release energy to make up the shortage. To gain weight, you must take in more calories than your total daily energy need.

One pound of fat has the energy value of about 3,500 calories. Thus, to lose one pound of weight, you must supply your body with 3,500 *fewer calories* than your total daily energy need.

For example, if you are sedentary and your desirable body weight is 125 pounds, your total daily energy need is 1,800 calories. You will lose a pound a week if you reduce your caloric intake to 1,300 calories per day.

Generally, you can safely create a deficit of 500 to 800 calories daily. It is not wise to create a daily deficit of more than 1,000 calories.

The daily energy need depends upon involuntary as well as voluntary activity of the body. Involuntary activity includes automatic actions, such as breathing, heart action, and keeping muscles alert so that they can act upon command. The daily energy need for involuntary activity—often referred to as the basal metabolic rate—is 10 to 12 calories for each pound of body weight, or 1,250 to 1,500 calories per day.

The energy requirement for voluntary activity depends on the size and number of muscles used and how long and strenuously you use them. For instance, the farther you walk is more important in burning up calories than the speed at which you walk. In other words, you'll use up more calories walking five miles at a moderate rate than walking fast for two miles.

A 120-pound woman using a standard typewriter will use 15 calories more an hour than if an electric typewriter were used.

Below are average energy (calorie) requirements for one hour of different activities. Certain activities, however, won't last an hour—dressing, for instance, or walking upstairs, or downstairs, or sprinting.

Activity	Calories per hour
Sleeping	70
Sitting or reading	77.4
Playing cards	91.8
Writing	132
Driving a car	168
Showering, shaving, or dressing	204
Walking	210
Walking downstairs	428.4
Walking upstairs	1114.8
Running cross country	636
Running long distance	900
Sprinting	1398
Dancing—disco	900
Swimming—breast stroke	
20 yd./min.	300
crawl, 45 yd./min.	690
Calisthenics	300
Bicycling—level roads	350
Tennis	426
Bowling	470
Volleyball	210
Golf	250--300
Ping pong	294
Squash	610

CHECK YOUR CHART BEFORE YOU EAT

Here is a small table to help you remember how long it actually takes to work off those extra calories.

	Cal.	Seated at a Desk Doing Paperwork	Walking or Standing
1 teaspoon sugar	15	10 minutes	3-8 minutes
1 slice white bread	60	40 minutes	12-20 minutes
1 medium apple	70	50 minutes	13-20 minutes
8 ounces of cola	95	1 hour	18-40 minutes
2 slices of bacon	100	1 hour	18-40 minutes

	Cal.	Seated at a Desk Doing Paperwork	Walking or Standing
1 doughnut	125	1½ hours	25–50 minutes
12 ounces of beer	150	1¾ hours	35–55 minutes
1 frankfurter	155	2 hours	½–1 hour
1 cup milk	160	2 hours	½–1 hour
3 ounces of hamburger (broiled)	250	3 hours	1–1½ hours

Source: Nutritive value from *Home and Garden Bulletin*, U.S. Department of Agriculture, rev. 1964.

Exercise for Working Beauty

Today's working woman is concerned about her physical fitness and is convinced that exercise is essential for a healthy, vigorous, productive life. But the efforts of most women are too irregular and too feeble to bring success. About half of the population—almost 100 million—say that they know they should exercise more.

WHY IS FITNESS IMPORTANT ON THE JOB?

Most jobs don't require brute strength. Why do we worry about strength and endurance in a pushbutton age? Well, paradoxically, exercise and fitness are especially of value when the physical demands of living are minimal. Here are some of the reasons:

- Strength and endurance help you to perform daily tasks with ease.
- Skill and agility minimize the effort required to do routine tasks.
- Poise and grace, important factors in your appearance, are by-products of physical fitness. They help you to feel at ease under work pressures and in social situations.
- Good muscle tone and posture can protect you from back problems that can be caused by repetitive activity or sitting all day.
- Physical activity helps in preventing degenerative diseases and many mental disorders.
- Exercise can also provide relief from tension and serves as a safe and natural tranquilizer.
- Feeling physically fit builds your self-concept. You need to see yourself at your optimum in as many ways as possible.
- Fitness protects you against accidents and may be a lifesaver in emergencies.

Exercising also increases muscle strength and endurance. It improves the functioning of the lungs, heart, blood vessels, brings up the body temperature, makes the joints more flexible, aids in weight control, and can have a positive effect on your complexion—clearing pimples for acne sufferers, and stimulating a youthful glow for those with dry or aging skin.

Lack of exercise has been cited as the cause of "creeping flab"—that subtle loss of muscle tone. It can be a problem for women who have the most slender figures. The breakdown of muscle tone and the accumulation of fat and water that lead to cellulite can affect the sparest of legs and thighs.

There are some basic misconceptions about exercise that prevent most people from enjoying it. And often these misconceptions are used as an excuse for not exercising. The two most common are: It takes too much time to exercise, and exercise really has less effect on the figure than dieting.

How much you exercise does affect the results you get. And actually there is precious little time. The American Medical Association recommends 30 to 60 minutes of exercise a day, or at least three times a week.

BASIC EXERCISES

The following are some exercises for general warm-up and conditioning that have been tested by the U.S. government. They can be done before work each day, or just before you make dinner in the evening.

Back Stretch: Stand erect, feet shoulder-width apart, arms extended over head. Stretch as high as possible, keeping heels on ground. Hold for 15 to 30 counts.

Reach and Bend: Stand erect, feet shoulder-width apart, arms at sides. Slowly bend over, touching the ground between the feet (or reach as far as you can go). Keep the knees flexed. Hold for 15 to 30 counts. Repeat 2 to 3 times.

Knee Pulls: Lie on back, feet extended, arms at sides. Pull one leg to chest, grasp with both arms and hold for 5 counts. Repeat with opposite leg. Repeat 7 to 10 times with each leg. Now try these: Lie on back, feet extended, hands at sides. Pull both legs to chest, lock arms around legs, pull buttocks slightly off ground. Hold for 20 to 40 counts. Repeat 7 to 10 times.

Twist: Lie on back, knees bent, feet on the ground, fingers interlaced behind neck. Curl torso to upright position and twist, touching the right knee with the left elbow. Return to starting position. Repeat, twisting in the opposite direction. Exhale on the way up, inhale on the way down. Repeat 5 to 15 series. For best effects, tuck your feet under a bed or sofa to prevent them from lifting during action.

Body Curl: Lie on back, legs straight, arms at sides. Curl head and shoulders off floor; hold this position for 5 counts. Return to starting position. Repeat 10 times.

Situp, Arms Crossed: Lie on back, arms crossed on chest, hands grasping opposite shoulders. Curl up to sitting position. Curl down to starting position. Repeat 10 times.

Situp, Fingers Laced: Lie on back, legs extended and feet spread one foot apart, fingers interlaced behind neck. Curl up to sitting position and touch right elbow to left knee. Curl down to sitting position. Curl up to sitting position and touch left elbow to right knee. Curl down to starting position. Repeat 15 times.

Arm Exercises

Horizontal Arm Circles: Stand erect, arms extended sideways at shoulder height, palms up. Make small circles backward with hands and arms. Reverse, turn palms down and do small circles forward. Repeat 15 times.

Giant Arm Circles: Stand erect, feet shoulder-width apart, arms at sides. Bring arms upward and sideways, crossing overhead, completing a full arc in front of body. Do equal number in each direction. Repeat 10 times.

Leg Exercises

When doing these exercises, keep the back straight. Start with the Knee Pushup and continue for several weeks until your stomach muscles are toned up enough to keep your back straight.

Knee Pushup: Lie prone, hands outside shoulders, fingers pointing forward, knees bent. Straighten arms, keeping back straight. Return to starting position. Repeat 5 times.

Pushup: Lie prone, hands outside shoulders, fingers pointing forward, feet on floor. Straighten arms, keeping back straight. Return to starting position. Repeat 10 times.

Quarter Knee Bends: Stand erect, hands on hips, feet

comfortably spaced. Bend knees to 45°, keeping heels on floor. Count 2; return to starting position. Repeat 15 times.

Sitting Single Leg Raises: Sit erect, hands on sides of chair seat for balance, legs extended at angle to floor. Raise left leg waist-high. Return to starting position. Repeat with opposite leg. Repeat 10 times with each leg.

Side Lying Leg Lift: Lie on right side, legs extended. Raise left leg as high as possible. Lower to starting position. Repeat on opposite side. Repeat 10 times.

Back Leg Swing: Stand erect behind chair, feet together, hands on chair for support. Lift one leg back and up as far as possible. Return to starting position. Repeat equal number of times with other leg. Repeat 20 times.

Heel Raises: Stand erect, hands on hips, feet together. Raise body on toes. Return to starting position. Repeat 20 times.

These exercises might best be done outside the actual nine-to-five work routine. The following exercises are activities that can and should be done during the day, as often as possible. Many of them are suitable to be done—quietly—at your desk in full view of everyone.

ON-THE-JOB EXERCISES

To Tone Your Waist, Arms, and Shoulders: Put your fingers under your desk, palms up. Try to lift the desk. And, while lifting, contract your stomach until the muscles are as tight and firm as possible. Count to 3 very slowly. Relax.

If you drive a great deal, tighten your stomach muscles every time you stop for a red light. Hold until the light turns green. You'll be surprised how this small exercise will really help in daily toning.

This next exercise can be done next to your desk. Spread your feet slightly, so they are about a foot-length apart. Slowly bend over (you can pretend you are picking up a paper). Don't bounce, just bend as slowly as possible while keeping your muscles firm. Slowly straighten up, and then bend again, very slowly. Keep bending, slowly. Now to one side, then the other. Try to keep your movements graceful and controlled.

These exercises are especially good for typists and women who are seated much of the day.

For Shoulders, Arms, and Breasts: Bend your elbows and grasp your wrists tightly. Lift your arms so your hands are about 10 inches away from your body. Push, arm against arm, as hard as possible. Push, hold for a count of 5, and then relax. Repeat at least 10 times and repeat as often as possible.

Place your hands on your shoulders, right hand on right shoulder, left on left shoulder. Now raise your arms to shoulder height. Try to touch your elbows in front, and then in back. This is similar to swinging your arms in wide circles, but it doesn't take as much room, and it is not very noticeable.

Stretch, just raising the arms, reaching to the ceiling, and straining to get as high as you can. Your posture and your chin will also benefit from trying to point your chin at the ceiling several times a day.

For Inner Thighs and Legs: Firming this part of the body is difficult even in a gym. For those who have to work in exercises while at work, it really requires concentration. Most daily activities only exercise the front and the back of the leg, and even climbing stairs does not exercise the inner thigh. You will need some file cabinets for this, or a high counter.

Hold the handle of the top file of a four- or five-drawer heavy metal file case, raise your right leg, with the knee straight, turning your leg and foot outward as high as you can. Hold the foot up, as high as possible, and count slowly to 5. Lower leg slowly and relax. Repeat at least 5 times for each leg.

Any activity that relaxes and loosens muscles that might get tense as you sit or stand in one position is good. Running in place, stretching, binding, moving your upper or lower body from side to side, any and all of these are helpful.

Movement can firm your body, and it can also get rid of nervous tension. Budget Rent-A-Car has recommended the following exercises for people who drive a great deal. This goes for anyone who is seated most of the day. Mind you, if you are doing the exercises in your car, it must be parked.

- Place both hands behind your head, interlace fingers. Push your head backward against your hands, but resist the motion with your hands. Count to 5. Relax.
- Place flattened palms, fingers pointing upward, against your forehead. The heels of your hands should be over each eyebrow. Keeping your eyes forward and neck very firm and straight, push your head against

the heels of your hands. Push, and resist, push and resist. Repeat 5 times. Relax.

- Place your left hand, flat against the left side of your head. Push your head toward your left shoulder, pushing out and down. Push, count to 5, relax. Repeat the exercise using the hand resistance against the right side of your head.
- Rotate your neck by turning your head first to the left, then right, then left again. Relax your head against your shoulder. Repeat.
- If you find your back becoming tired and your shoulders strained, this exercise will loosen and relax the important muscles of the lower back. Remaining seated, place feet flat on the floor, or on the floor of the car. Droop your entire body first to the right side, and then to the left. Allow yourself to be completely limp. Don't force or bounce, just droop. Hold the position with your arms dangling on the floor for about two seconds; rise slowly. Relax, and repeat.

Do the exercises suggested here, or ones that you develop yourself, every day at a specific time. You'll feel better for it, and you'll enjoy a surge of energy after each exercise session.

Exercise, by itself, will not really make you lose weight or become exquisitely trim and fit unless you spend a great deal of time at it. But, exercise will give you self-confidence in your own body. It will allow you to "feel" yourself move, act, and react. You are a *force*; that knowledge is important to you in competitive work situations.

9
5
Keeping Up
Moving Up

Making Your Work Environment Beautiful

Birds, orangutans, and even fish all want to have a space of their own; a place to feel comfortable and secure. People want the same thing. Your desk, your work station, and your "area" represent you. It is surprising how many chic, well-groomed women have offices that are cluttered with pictures of pets and old boyfriends, out-of-date newspapers and magazines, and sick plants. Your office, work station, or even locker, are you. Make no mistake: Management and co-workers react negatively to personal mess like soggy tissues in your desk drawer, and are very observant and critical of your personal-area cleaning.

LOOK OVER YOUR SPACE

Estimate the space that is assigned to you. Most Americans, you'll notice, rarely stand closer than three feet, even when in an intense conversation. Your work area should give you at least that amount of space for ease of movement, and also for psychic security. Is your space exactly like that of dozens of others? Is all the furniture the same? Do other employees share chairs, file cases, or work tables with you? Draw a chart that shows your area, in scale, and place a small circle to represent you, where you stand, or sit, most of the time. It will give you a sort of map of your location.

Most American offices have a private drawer, locker, or

cabinet for you to keep your personal objects. If your company doesn't, suggest they do. The secure locker will mean a great deal to you, and to the other employees.

If you are an executive, or have a private office or work space, be sure that your office is equal to or better than the office of any male counterpart at your level. If it isn't — do something about it immediately.

If you are a new employee, you'll have a better chance of changing your environment than if you've endured depressing, uncomfortable, or unattractive facilities for any length of time. But if you have, and feel that a change is overdue, devise a plan that will accomplish the change you want. (Make sure it will also achieve an outcome that is desirable for several other people, too.)

If you are in a draft, too cold, too warm, or perhaps worst of all, in an airless area, complain bitterly. Make sure your complaints emphasize increased productivity as a result of better ventilation. Bad air, uncomfortable temperatures, and other ventilation problems are beauty enemies. Luckily, women seem to be able to endure relatively high temperatures and still continue to work well, if not comfortably. However, the new energy problems mean that most work areas will be cooler than comfortable for seated work.

TIPS ON KEEPING WARM IN YOUR OFFICE

Wear several layers of loose-fitting clothing; layering keeps body heat in and lets body perspiration out. Napped, piled, and textured fabrics retain heat. Cotton is the best fabric to wear next to the skin; it will absorb perspiration and keep you comfortable. (Layered under a light sweater, it will keep you warm and dry.) Wear a suit jacket if possible. It will make you look very businesslike and will keep you warm. Or wear sweaters and sweater sets, which are newly popular again.

The color of the walls around you reflects on your skin. A blue or purple background is not as flattering as sunny yellow or pink. Unfortunately, warm light colors are seldom used by industrial designers. If you have a choice, select a warm cheerful color, like coral. If you cannot select the wall covering, a giant poster or open landscape can visually enlarge your work area.

Avoid pictures, clippings, and personal notes thumbtacked to walls or taped to your work area. The walls around your work area shouldn't look like a teenager's bulletin board. If you have children or grandchildren, carry their pictures in your wallet. There are exceptions: political pictures showing you with the president of the United States, or a picture of you with Robert Redford or Paul Newman.

Keep your desk as clean and attractive as possible. It doesn't mean that your desk top should be compulsively paper-free, only that it looks as if you can find something if you are looking for it. Your desk lamp or work light should be at a convenient angle so that it illuminates your work area and reflects attractively on your complexion. If you can, use pink light bulbs; they reflect beautifully and are flattering to most complexions.

If you work under harsh, unattractive fluorescent lighting, use a slightly rosier foundation than you would for normal or outdoor use. It counters the color-draining effect of the flickering lighting.

Make sure your chair is comfortable. Don't just adjust your body to the work conditions; try to adjust the situation to you so that you can perform most effectively.

In many offices, the height of the back of the chair indicates status. It is too bad, because actually secretarial chairs are the best support for your back and the most comfortable for all-day sitting, and years of striving can end in a backache.

While your work area is yours alone, it should also be inviting to others. You should provide a big ashtray, even if you don't smoke; a clock if it is convenient; and, of course, a telephone.

Your telephone, at work, if it is on your desk, should be immaculately clean. You can clean it with a bit of cotton soaked in your cologne. It will get rid of any residue that might build up on the phone, and the slight scent that lingers can make talking nice.

A word about work space: Your work space is yours; don't hesitate to excuse yourself from unwelcome or time-wasting visitors and politely go back to work. To paraphrase a very wise woman: More careers have been destroyed by gossip than by bad breath.

A FULL-LENGTH MIRROR

Check in your office to see if a full-length mirror can be installed in the ladies' room. Even if several women have to chip in to buy an inexpensive mirror, it is worth it. Keep yourself — your total image — in mind when you dress; adjust your hose and clothes carefully after using the facilities.

Now that you have an office mirror and your work area is attractive and comfortable, it is a perfect frame for your special kind of beauty, and should enable you to look your best all day.

Beauty and the Business Trip

The number of women traveling for business, or as salespeople, or for conventions is increasing three times as fast as the number of traveling businessmen. Airlines, hotel chains, and travel agents have become aware of the need to provide special services for traveling women, and many of them will provide booklets or information suited to the woman traveler's needs.

THE BASICS

Business travel means a different kind of planning than for vacations. It means being with the same people, if you are at a convention, and having to be alert and ready to think and act fast—at all times.

Airline baggage regulations permit you to check two bags through for domestic flights. The domestic airlines allow you to carry on a 9" x 12" x 23" case that fits under the seat and a garment bag for your longer garments, as well as a coat and a briefcase, and of course, your handbag. When the plane lands, you'll be ready to go on your way without the waiting for baggage. You should be able to pack everything you'll need for a week, or even two weeks, in a small carry-on bag, and a briefcase.

Your carry-on bag should include several small kits with all the essentials for civilized living and beauty:

- toothpaste
- toothbrush
- dental floss

- travel alarm (you can usually call the front desk if you forget your own clock)
- deodorant
- small razor or depilatory cream
- travel robe or covering robe or coat
- shower cap
- aspirins, vitamins, or prescription medication
- Band-Aids and sanitary supplies
- extra glasses or contacts, or your prescription sunglasses
- shampoo, cream rinse, conditioner, a portable dryer, electric rollers or curlers, pins, brushes, combs, and barrettes

In your large travel handbag you can carry the following personal materials:

- special soap and cleanser
- astringents, moisturizer, night cream, or oil-rich cream to counteract the drying effects of travel
- hand lotion and petroleum jelly are always useful

Your makeup kit should include small amounts of:
- foundation
- rouge or blusher
- eyebrow pencils
- eyeliner
- mascara
- tweezers, nail scissors, clippers
- lipstick or color pot
- lip brush, lip liner
- emery board
- nail enamel, enamel remover, orange stick
- moist towelettes
- perfume

Your clothes-care equipment should also be in your handbag, because emergencies can take place when en route.
That kit should include:

- sewing kit
- spot-remover pads
- detergent or soap flakes
- plastic hangers; a small string for hanging
- clothes brush or a small roll of clear plastic tape (the tape is great for hems and as a lint remover)

- plastic bags
- shoe polish in small packets
- safety pins

     Your now-full handbag should include work-necessities, too.

- address book
- agenda for any business conference
- note pad and pen
- stamps and self-addressed envelopes
- small folding umbrella or rain-repellent scarf

     Many women keep these essentials with them at all times. It's easy enough to manage all of this if you group everything in sandwich-sized plastic bags, or in small makeup cases.

     To keep yourself fit while you travel, remember that large hotels, and even some smaller ones, have swimming pools and saunas for the convenience of their guests. And if you take along a small swimsuit, you'll find it is possible to make use of these relaxing facilities.

PACKING TO GO

Packing is one of the lesser arts. But it is an art. You can learn the "layer system" that works best for most women. At the bottom, place all the heavy and bulky items. The heaviest objects should be placed along the sides and over the hinges, opposite the handles. If you position heavy materials this way, they won't shift when the case is carried.

     Separate the layers of material with lightweight cardboard cut to the size of the case. The cardboard provides a firming surface that makes packing easier. If you have a soft cloth case, you can buy some padded mailing bags at your local stationery store and you can pack these full of crushable garments or clothes that should not be squashed.

- Stuff shoes with nightclothes or lingerie.
- Stuff extra purses full of blouses, pantyhose, or other small items of clothing
- Put shoes in large socks. You can use the socks as slippers, too.
- Remove detachable belts and pins from dresses, and empty the pockets of slacks and jackets before packing.

- Keep similar things together; you can find everything you need with just one hunt.
- Pack a gold belt or scarf, and a dressy purse. It can turn a dark blouse and skirt into an evening outfit. Gold or silver sandals can make everything—from a simple tweed to a cotton dress—look very dressed-up.
- When you fold clothes, fold at the waist and shoulder along the natural body lines if possible. Roll skirts lengthwise. Tissue paper is still the best protection against wrinkles.
- Pack heavy things like books or electric curlers near the hinges of your bag, or what would be the bottom of the bag.
- Liquids should be put in plastic bottles, but don't fill the bottles more than three-fourths full; squeeze the extra air out before sealing. To be on the double-safe side, pack the bottles inside a small plastic bag.
- Carry a small tape recorder with you. It will help you organize details, and you'll be prepared for any business negotiations or sales closings.
- Use your business card to identify your luggage. Never put your home address on your bags; it announces to thieves that you'll be away from your home for a while.
- If you pick up extra clothes or materials you don't want to carry, you can always use the mailers to send yourself a package.

   The chart below shows a basic three-, four-, or five-day business trip wardrobe. It is based on travel in the fall, winter, and early spring of most of the United States. You can add to it to make it suitable for a week's trip or adapt the basic wardrobe for warm climates by changing the fabrics.

Basics	Formal	Informal
	(Key letters to code listed below)	
Lightweight coat Raincoat Poncho or cape	B, D, or F with skirt from suit	I, H, A for a walk or side trip
Gray or beige suit Black or navy blazer with solid skirt	A, B, D, with F D with skirt and J or K	A, C, with E and G; jacket with I & H; D can be layered
Silk blouse and skirt Jersey or soft fabric dress	F, J, and K	D, E, J

Accessories:

A   Turtle or cowl-neck sweater
B   Soft silk or light dressy blouse
C   Tailored shirt, or cotton blouse
D   Tight black t-shirt or thin sweater
E   Walking shoes with medium heels, pumps
F   Sandals or dressy shoes
G   Heavy socks (knee-length), or boots (if you have lots of space for packing them)
H   Flat shoes, loafers, or sneakers
I   Jeans (thin cotton or lightweight corduroy)
J   Scarfs, solid silk and wool
K   Gold belts, evening purse, dressy jewelry

A Checklist of Clothing

This list is included to help you organize your clothing and accessories:

- Casual dress for day
- Dressier dress for dinner
- Slacks or jeans
- Skirt (solids work best)
- Suit with skirt or slacks (medium-tone blazer or extra jacket)
- Blouse, shirts, sweater
- Sportswear, such as swimsuit or tennis dress
- Coat, jacket, rainwear, stole, or cape
- Robes, gown, or pajamas
- Bras, panties, slips, petticoats
- Pantyhose
- Heeled shoes
- Flat shoes, slippers
- Boots
- Jewelry, belts, scarves
- Cosmetics kit
- Bright yellow plastic rain jacket or poncho

Women who travel frequently naturally have the best suggestions:

Dorothy Fuller, the fashion director for the Apparel Center in Chicago, says: "I start by asking myself, what am I going to do on this trip?" She studies her agenda and lays out the clothing and accessories that go together. Then she says, "I mentally go through each day. Then I go back again to the packing and simplify as much as possible. Personally, I prefer to travel at night. My travel outfit might be navy flannel slacks, a camel-hair blouson, and a camel poncho. Then, when I arrive, I put that outfit away, and don't look at it again until it is time to fly back." Ms. Fuller says that sometimes her work outfits are jeans and sneakers, but she advises, "When you're in public, you should look well put together. . . . If you're going to make a special deal, or want to make a special impression, you want to be sure your outfit really works for you." That motto is especially true when you are traveling. You will be on display everywhere, and you'll have to look perfect for hours, without a convenient spot to freshen up.

MAKE SURE THAT TRAVEL ISN'T BROADENING

Getting appropriate exercise is another important consideration while traveling.

Isometric exercises and stress-chasing exercises such as the following can help keep you limber even after carrying heavy cases, or after sitting for hours.

Shrug your shoulders as high as possible. Relax them, and pull them down as you lift your head as high as possible. Repeat about 5 times.

Clasp hands, push against the opposite hand; pull back and forth, and then downward, and then push upward. Repeat several times.

Sit as far forward as possible. Grip hands behind your back. Pull up with the top hand and down with the other. You'll feel your back muscles working and then relaxing as you relax. Repeat this exercise as often as you like.

Grip your hands above your head (an inch or two would be fine); slowly, with as much tension as possible, bring the elbows together.

Sit with your back as straight and firm as possible. Point your chin at the ceiling. Open your mouth and relax your jaw, then clench. Repeat several times. Lower your head and relax. Repeat the entire exercise.

A final note about travel and beauty.

As pressurized cabins or air-conditioned automobiles mean dry air, carry a small jar or tube of moisturizer with you for covering your hands as well as your face and neck. Even if you have oily skin, you will notice dry lines when you travel.

Usually try to avoid new cosmetics and new foods when you travel for business. You don't know what will bring on an allergic reaction, or how your body will react to the additional strain of new food. Flight attendants and other professional travelers often advise eating less and drinking more water and fruit juices. Stick to light salads and fresh fruits for at least one meal during any conference. Avoid sauces and heavy or rich foods.

If you bring a small box of raisins, or a piece of fruit with you, you'll not be tempted to eat the foods served on planes or trains or at roadside fast-food stops. Be sure you drink at least one cup of water for each hour that you travel. It will make a big difference in the way you withstand everything from crossing time zones to being dried under lights and air-blasts on jumbo-jets, to being rattled on a fast-moving train, car, or bus.

Stress—Beauty's Worst Enemy

- A twenty-year-old woman learns her mentor in the office has just been fired.
- A saleswoman loses an important business deal to a competitor.
- A boutique owner cannot find a reliable supplier for her most popular item.
- A senior vice-president is finally offered stock options in a firm she has worked with for twenty years.

What do all these women and situations have in common? *Stress.*

WHAT IS STRESS?

Happy events can be as stressful as unhappy events. Events that cause intensity of feeling are called *stressors* by Dr. Hans Selye, who was the first to define and name the phenomenon.

The physical reaction to intense feeling is the same, regardless of the cause—pleasant or unpleasant. The only freedom from stress is death. But stress makes life more interesting. Even when you are asleep, your body functions continue and dreams can cause physical activity and mental or emotional stress. Interestingly, stress from emotional frustrations is more likely to produce disease than stress from physical exercise, such as jogging or dancing. A working woman often faces stress—twenty-four hours of unending stress—for weeks on end.

How can you tell if you suffer stress? If you're alive, you probably are dealing with stress. Regardless of the source of the stress, from a martinet, too much pressure, or even unfair politics in the office or workplace, your body will react in three classic stages.

First, there's *alarm*. Your body alerts itself by releasing hormones and your blood sugar goes up, releasing energy to your bloodstream. Your reaction is similar to the feeling you get when your boss criticizes you or humiliates you in front of other employees—a sick, shocked, and angry feeling. You start to sweat and your pupils dilate; you might feel a burst of angry energy or outright fury.

Then comes a second stage, when you fight back; this is called the *resistance* stage. The body tries to regulate itself and to repair any damage that the stressor might have caused, and your emotions struggle to regain their equilibrium. If the stress continues, your body has a hard time accepting the continued stress, and your body cannot repair itself when constantly on alert.

After the first two stages, the body is *exhausted*. This exhaustion causes the body to break down, and diseases—some known to be linked to stress, others only suspected—might appear. Headaches, especially migraine headaches in women, are linked to stress. Working women, who often must financially support children and aged parents, please bosses and supervisors, advance their own careers so that they can earn more money and attract more interesting work, and still function as attractive women in a society that judges women on how they look, might easily be in the first or second stage of stress for hours every day.

FIGHTING STRESS

Physical activity is one of the best ways to combat stress. When tension mounts and everything seems to be going wrong, and the stress seems unbearable, you can do the following exercise to help relieve the pressure. It's simple, and if you can breathe you can do it.

- Sit upright at your desk or station.
- Place your hands, fingers touching, in the middle of your midriff, over your stomach.
- Inhale slowly and deeply through your nose, pushing out the stomach with air-inflated lungs.
- Push hard against the fingers from the inside of your body. Fill your lungs completely.

- Hold for a count of 5.
- Relax and slowly exhale through your nose.
- As you empty your lungs, tighten your stomach muscles, and firm and lift the diaphragm.
- When your lungs are empty, repeat the procedure.

You've heard the expression, "Take a deep breath . . . and then go on." This deep breathing exercise will help you think clearly and also relax you.

Sleep is also important in dealing with stress. More than half of working women suffer from sleep problems. To get appropriate sleep, most doctors suggest increased physical activity and decreased mental activity before bedtime.

Don't go to bed until you really feel tired. If you lie awake in bed for more than a half hour, it will frustrate you and make you more anxious—adding fear of the exhaustion you'll be suffering the next day to whatever is already keeping you awake.

Try to set up a "sleepy-time" pattern by going to bed at the same time every night. You can establish pleasant routines with a warm bath, applying body lotion after the bath, and then relaxing with a book, or a very calming TV program. Something that takes little concentration. Milk actually does have sleep-inducing properties. It contains two established nerve-soothers—calcium and tryptophan, which is an essential amino acid.

If the warm bath, the relaxing thoughts, and the milk aren't enough, practice focusing your mind on certain areas of the body to bring their functions under conscious control. Lie on your back and put one hand over your midriff, between the waist and lower ribs. Then concentrate on relaxing: start with the eyes, then the jaws, the tongue, and the neck, then the shoulders, the arms, and the body. Keep concentrating on each part of the body until you feel the muscles soften and relax, and you are ready to roll over, to your most comfortable position, and drop off to sleep.

NIGHTLY SLEEP FOR DAILY BEAUTY

One or two nights without sleep can be disastrous for your appearance. After insufficient sleep, the chemical functions of the body lose their efficiency in converting food into energy. This slows down the process of cell renewal and the skin cells that normally act to keep our faces looking firm are not fed properly. Result: dull, sagging skin. As you do sleep, corisol, an adrenal hormone that contributes to the replenishing and refreshing of the skin, is released.

Every working woman should also schedule time for recreation and relaxation. You should keep reminding yourself that you *deserve* to relax and enjoy yourself.

When you're feeling anxious, restless, and unhappy, act—get out. Brooding will just make it worse. Do not go over and over a stressful situation—all the plans and calculations for career success do not automatically work. A schemer is obvious to everyone, and the stress of manipulating every situation is bound to wear on your looks. Instead, add to your knowledge: Learn how to play a musical instrument, or how to paint, or take some driving lessons.

On the other hand, there are dangerous ways of dealing with stress that should under all circumstances be avoided. Among them are tranquilizers, diet or sleeping pills, and alcohol. These just mask stress symptoms, so you cannot deal with them effectively.

There are an estimated 4 million women alcoholics in the United States. In the last few years, the number of women problem drinkers has doubled. If you are a working woman, the chances of using drink as a response to stress is increasing. Having a drink or two when you've had a bad day is a much-cherished ritual in the business world. Drinks at lunch and drinks after work are semi-social obligations in many creative jobs. But you don't *need* to drink.

Nor do you need to overwork to mask your feelings. Workaholics don't usually accomplish as much as they think they do, although their priority—work, and more work—can be as satisfying as any other.

What does the job mean? If you had a short time to live, would you continue working at it in the same way? Is the time and effort you put into your work really necessary, or is it a form of escape, and do you use work to fill another void in your life? Do you take work personally; do you feel that you're the only person who can be effective? And are you sure that your extra effort is not misread as an inability to handle your job?

The most important factor, however, in avoiding stress is really liking the work you do at your job.

When you like your work, it will show; you'll be excited

and stimulated by what you do. Each day will be fun and a challenge; you'll grow in confidence and be pleased to take on new assignments. And you'll actually become interested in the *subject* of the work. Really loving your work and having genuine interest is more attractive to management than sycophancy, mentor-mating, or any of the hundreds of power and status ploys that books, articles, and women's groups advise.

And finally, in avoiding stress realize that life is full of disappointments. And that coping with disappointments can make even unpleasant situations learning experiences, and you can benefit from them. Being passed over for a promotion or a pay raise, being fired, laid off, or suffering a lowering of your status—all of these can bring on feelings of dejection and misery. But here are a couple of steps that may make things easier:

- Talk it over with a friend who is outside the office. Someone who is really supportive. Listen to any thoughts your friend might have. But just the talking has a therapeutic value.
- Keep yourself physically active as well as mentally alert. If you've been fired, do something positive, like going rollerskating—it really does help. Just keep moving, and moving, until the initial pain stops.

OFFICE GOSSIP

One of the causes of stress is office gossip based on personality conflicts. It is easy to say ignore other people's manipulations or stories; it is hard to do when their actions can have a very real effect on your status, work assignments, and paycheck. You cannot really hold yourself aloof—by working in a group situation you are involved. All that you can do is be sure that your actions are consistent with your own code of ethics.

SEX

Sexual harassment can cause stress and anxiety, and a feeling of isolation because it is hard to talk about the subject. Just as you don't want to be pressured or coerced, don't play on the weaknesses of some men. If a man's ego desperately needs reassurances, he will be easy to convince with flattery. Being beautiful, intelligent, and in a career situation has its responsibilities —you can leap-frog into positions of prestige, but real power comes from ability and confidence; selection for your merit, not for your favors is what you want.

5 Appendix

A Personality Quiz That Will Tell You Something About Yourself

The idea of this book is to make you more beautiful and your work life better and happier.

Before you can really start on a new life, you must know exactly what you like about your old life and what is bothering you about it. To do this, answer the following exercises and quizzes with a *yes* or *no*. The tests are easy and entertaining, as well as diagnostic.

They are not, however, scientific, or reflective of every personality. But they will help each reader to get a better picture of herself. For before you can change, you must know how you actually behave.

Begin by looking over the following list and write the words that best describe you on a piece of paper. Then start from there. You cannot change, but you can modify your personality so that you function more effectively in society.

WHO ARE YOU?

POSITIVE	or	NEGATIVE
CALM AND RELAXED	or	NERVOUS AND HIGH-STRUNG
SHY AND RETIRING	or	BOLD, SURE OF YOURSELF

PASSIVE, GENTLE, KINDLY *or*   ASSERTIVE, AGGRESSIVE, BOSSY
TIMID, CAUTIOUS   *or*   BRAVE, FEARLESS, AND DRAMATIC

Remember that no matter who you are, it might not be you who are the problem, but the type of work or environment you place yourself in.

ARE YOU A POSITIVE OR NEGATIVE PERSON?

Answer *yes* or *no*. Try to be as honest as possible with your answers.

1. Is your health poor?
2. Do you often have mysterious aches and pains?
3. Do you suffer from stress?
4. Do you often have headaches?
5. Do you ever have dizzy spells?
6. Do you often have colds or coughs?
7. Do you sleep lightly?
8. Are you often tired, even in the morning?
9. Are you more than 10 pounds over or under weight?
10. Do you take any prescription medication?
11. Do you worry a great deal?
12. Are you frequently irritable?
13. Do you often feel lonely?
14. Are you often bored or restless?
15. Do you have any close friends?
16. Do you ever have arguments with your neighbors?
17. Are you very shy?
18. Do you frequently find your mind wandering?
19. Do you suffer from unexplained or unreasonable fears?
20. Do you ever feel guilty for no reason?
21. Do you feel that you are being criticized?
22. Do you have trouble communicating?
23. Are people often rude to you?
24. Do you feel that you have bad luck?
25. Are you ever angry with no apparent reason?
26. Do you feel that your life has been a failure?
27. Do you ever wish you "could do it over"?
28. Do you worry about the future?
29. Do you sometimes feel sad and melancholy?
30. Do you ever consider suicide?

If you have answered *yes* to more than 10 of these questions, you are somewhat serious. If you have answered *yes* to more than 20 of these questions, you are very negative. But if you have answered *yes* to less than 10 questions, you are usually a positive and optimistic person.

Are You Calm or Nervous?

The following quiz is designed to find out if you are for the most part a relaxed person or a nervous person. Some people who are very nervous really don't know how they seem to other people, and don't realize that they are agitated so often. Answer yes or no to each of the following questions:

1. Do you often worry about money? _____
2. Do you worry about the future? _____
3. Do you often give parties or entertain friends? _____
4. Do you ever wake up in the middle of the night with a worry? _____
5. Do you ever feel that you "just can't go on?" _____
6. Do you ever feel that you cannot cope with a situation? _____
7. Do you often feel nervous? _____
8. Do you drink more than four cups of coffee a day? _____
9. Do you have to do everything in a special manner or order? _____
10. Do you suffer from constipation? _____
11. Do you often suffer from diarrhea? _____
12. Do you often have dizzy spells? _____
13. Do you find that your heart races or palpitates when you have not been running or exercising? _____
14. Do you smoke more than ten cigarettes a day? _____
15. Is there some habit that you have been unable to break? _____
16. Do you overreact to small mishaps? _____
17. Do you often feel unable to make a decision? _____
18. Do you sometimes feel at a loss for words? _____
19. Do you worry constantly? _____
20. Are you afraid of the dark? _____
21. Do you become very angry if you are caught in traffic or are forced to wait on line? _____
22. Do you often worry about your health? _____
23. Do you stutter, stammer, or repeat phrases? _____
24. When making introductions, do you often forget names? _____
25. Do your lips, hand, or knees tremble for no reason? _____
26. Do you ever feel a constriction in your chest? _____
27. Are you afraid of flying? _____
28. Do you sweat profusely? _____
29. Do you fear you have bad breath or body odor? _____
30. Do you often feel you just cannot cope?

If you have answered yes to fewer than 10 of these questions, you are usually calm and poised; however, if you have answered yes to more than 20 of these questions, you are a nervous person, and you might want to seek professional help. You are suffering needlessly.

Are You Shy or Bold?

The following quiz is designed to tell if you are daring, self-confident, and active, or plagued with doubts and rather retiring. Everyone suffers from moments—or times—of self-doubt and feelings of inadequacy. But, before you can act against those feelings, you must objectively realize that you suffer, perhaps more than most people, from these tendencies.

1. Do you ever feel that life is "just too much"?   _____
2. Do you have trouble accepting criticism?   _____
3. Do you have to brag to strangers because otherwise you think they will not treat you well?   _____
4. Do you think you are ugly?   _____
5. Are you proud of your family?   _____
6. Do you wish your friends would be more supportive?   _____
7. Are you often lonely?   _____
8. Do you feel sure of failure, before you even begin?   _____
9. Do you feel someone else could probably do your job better?   _____
10. Do you daydream often?   _____
11. Do you sometimes feel uncomfortable in your surroundings?   _____
12. Do you worry that people may be gossiping about you?   _____
13. Do you feel uncomfortable with strangers?   _____
14. Do you hate to see yourself in photographs?   _____
15. Do you recognize your own voice on a recording?   _____
16. Do you sometimes feel you are a failure?   _____
17. Are you unsatisfied with your achievements?   _____
18. Do you ever wish you were someone else?   _____
19. Do you hesitate to express your opinions?   _____
20. Do you ever envy others and feel life is easier for others?   _____
21. Do you dread the thought that others will disappoint you?   _____
22. Do you think that you've been forgotten if your friends are late for a date?   _____
23. Do you doubt you are attractive to the opposite sex?   _____
24. Do you ever feel your gestures are gross or vulgar?   _____
25. Do you change your clothes often before leaving the house?   _____
26. Do you buy clothes or household possessions to impress others?   _____
27. Do you worry if you are not in fashion?   _____
28. Do you check the mirror often, and worry about how you look?   _____
29. Do you change your hair style often?   _____
30. Do you wear more than the usual amount of makeup?   _____

If you answered yes to more than 10 of these questions you are very shy and lack self-confidence. If you answered yes to fewer than 10 questions, you are self-confident, and if you answered *yes* to fewer than 5 you are quite bold. If this is the case, perhaps you should worry more about others' feelings.

Are You Passive or Aggressive? *(turtle or skunk)*

The following is designed to help you see yourself as others see you — as a passive or aggressive person; or perhaps in between. Do you find yourself often in arguments, and do you usually take the offensive? Or, do you try to avoid conflict, and sometimes even back away from what you know is right — just to avoid an argument?

1. Do you always start arguments? _____
2. When you are losing an argument, do you resort to tears, or shout, or call names? _____
3. Do you go back to an argument, even when the subject has been changed? _____
4. Do you carry grudges? _____
5. Do you hate to lose at games? _____
6. Are you a good competitor, even when you are losing? _____
7. Do you find it difficult to deal with irritating people? _____
8. Do you think of "getting even" when you feel wronged? _____
9. Are you quick to correct people? _____
10. Are you critical of people who you feel are lazy or stupid? _____
11. If someone is rude to you, do you immediately retaliate? _____
12. Do you belong to any social clubs or groups? _____
13. Do you speak up when someone gets in front of you on line? _____
14. Have you ever complained to an authority figure when you felt a situation at work was unpleasant? _____
15. Do you welcome responsibility? _____
16. Would you do almost anything to avoid an "ugly scene"? _____
17. Do you hate to give orders? _____
18. Would you rather do something yourself than ask someone to do it for you? _____
19. Do you feel responsible, at a party, for everyone's enjoying themselves, even if you are not the hostess? _____
20. Do you find yourself offering to do menial tasks? _____
21. Has a pushy salesperson ever pressured you into buying something you really didn't want? _____
22. Do you tend to agree with people? _____
23. Do you lie when you are in an unpleasant situation? _____
24. Do you feel responsible for everything—even bad weather? _____
25. Do you allow others to cheat at games? _____
26. Have you ever accused anyone of being a liar? _____

27. Do you suspect your spouse or lover of being unfaithful, but will not confront him or her?   _____
28. Do you become upset if you hear about violence or torture?   _____
29. Do you feel incapable of violence?   _____
30. Do you suffer from migraine headaches?   _____

You may notice that the type of questions varied from numbers 1 through 15 and 16 through 30. If you answered yes to more than five of numbers 1 through 15, you are probably quite assertive and able to defend yourself. If you answered yes to more than 10 questions, many people might consider you very aggressive. If most of your answers to questions 16 through 30 were yes, you are probably a passive person. But you might be very angry, about many things — underneath. Controlling your anger may not always be good. Very often repressed anger can result in sleepless nights, headaches, and many kinds of diseases. Unresolved anger and the resulting stress that it puts on your body is not good for your health. Many women are passive by nature, but in order to operate in society, you must be able to react to unpleasant situations.

Are You Brave or Cautious?

The following quiz is designed to find out if you take risks. Risks are part of working life and venturing out; every day—especially if you are interested in your career and making changes in your life—requires a certain kind of bravery. No, not the bravery that makes you a hero, and that sends people into burning buildings to rescue a loved one or a stranger. It is the bravery to change and to accept the possibility of rejection and of failure.

1. On a cold day, do you never leave the house without a coat?   _____
2. Do you always carry an umbrella at the slightest chance of rain?   _____
3. Do you pay your bills immediately?   _____
4. Do you fear the ringing of the telephone late at night?   _____
5. Is security an important part of your lifestyle?   _____
6. Would you move to a new city or community for a better job?   _____
7. Do you carefully save money, often denying yourself things you need?   _____

8. Do you consider a pension very important? _____
9. Do you check and recheck your personal finances? _____
10. Do you avoid going to the doctor because of the bills? _____
11. Do you ever bet on horseraces or games? _____
12. Do you invest in the stock market? _____
13. Do you enjoy taking small risks such as buying a dress that is on sale without trying it on? _____
14. Do you carefully read your mail? _____
15. Have you ever felt defrauded in a business venture? _____
16. Do you often call your lawyer? _____
17. Are you always on time for trains? _____
18. Do you prefer games without scores or betting? _____
19. Are you terrified on airplanes or fast cars? _____
20. Do you always wear a safety belt when you are in a car? _____
21. Do you always check the lights before crossing the street? _____
22. Do you enjoy looking at things from a great height? _____
23. Do you have abnormal fears of any sort? _____
24. Do you feel anxious if you don't do the same thing, at the same time, every day? _____
25. Do you have a fire alarm in your home? _____
26. Do you always caution people you love to be "careful" when they leave the house? _____
27. At a restaurant, do you ever worry about food poisoning? _____
28. Do you fear that you are victim to some strange disease? _____
29. Do you loathe speaking up, even when you see an injustice? _____
30. Do you try to get a favorable relationship with an authority figure? _____

If you answered yes to more than 8 of these questions you are a very careful person, probably very conservative. However, if you answered *no* to all of the questions, you often "leap before you look" and you might be well-advised to act with more caution.

WHAT DO THE QUIZZES MEAN?

The best way to look your best at work is to feel secure and confident. That comes only with self-knowledge and the satisfaction of doing a job well.

When at work, take each new task and judge it against your personality and your natural talents. It is only sensible to do the kind of work that fits you best. Unpleasant jobs can sometimes be rearranged and re-thought to make them do-able, if not completely fun. But first, you must know yourself.

Quick Tips for On-the-Job Beauty

TIPS AND TRICKS

Why is it that sometimes you need to have a quick remedy? Oh, it is super to work at your makeover and to know that it really fits you and is part of you, but there are times when everyone needs immediate help—something like a life buoy. The following are a list of emergency aids, followed by tips and tricks that are time and work savers—and beauty aids.

Emergency Measures

Be prepared: Always carry a 1" x 1" card with white, beige, and black thread wound around it and a needle stuck securely in the card. I keep mine in a matchbook, after removing the matches.

    If a blemish seems about to appear, or your face seems blotchy, hold an ice-cold piece of water-soaked paper toweling against your face.

    If you are in a ladies' room and there are no towels, don't panic—it is better for your face if it dries naturally (apply moisturizer to damp face).

    If you feel exhausted and tired, dangle your hands under cool running water.

Nails

Apply nail polish at night, at least twelve hours before you use your hands.

    Color the inside of a long nail on the extended part with clear polish; it helps to strengthen the nail.

    Rub one capsule of vitamin E into your cuticles for a rich

healthful finger smoother. Push cuticles back with wood or plastic, never metal.

Don't match your nail color to your lipstick; match it to your hand size, shape, and your personality. Also consider your use of hand gestures; more gesture, less color.

You can create extra glitter for a fast change from work to a party evening by brushing frosted shadow over wet nail enamel and then covering with a clear coat.

Outdoor Work

Don't use perfume if you work in the sun; a chemical reaction with the sun can stain the skin.

A cooling quick masque of yogurt, vinegar, tea, or witch hazel are all good for easing and calming heat-red skin.

Your Body

Weight gains and losses of over ten pounds strain your skin as well as your internal organs.

Exercise at your desk by keeping things in inconvenient places.

Wear sunglasses indoors if you are bothered by glare.

Smoking causes a contraction in the muscles around the eyes, and encourages wrinkles.

Cod-liver oil is one of the best A and D vitamin sources possible. Don't forget brewer's yeast for vitamin B. If you skip lunch, remember vitamins.

When selecting glasses, the top of the frame should cover your brows, the bottom extend past your eye bone.

Climb stairs as often as possible; don't use the elevator for less than five flights.

Clear lip gloss can be used around your eyes to ward off drying effects of wind. Squinting into the wind causes tension lines.

Exercise your toes by taking your shoes off and wiggling your toes under your desk.

Never go an entire day without a bra—no matter how firm you are; a bra helps you stay that way.

Hair

Keep hair covered in cold weather, but always avoid tight or binding headwear. Never wear a close-fitting cloche or plastic rainhat.

Arrange hair with fingers before combing. It will avoid many of the tangles.

Ribbon curlers can give you the softest lightest set. Just knot the ribbon around the ends of the hair and roll; and tie in a bunch at the scalp. If you do this neatly, you can go to work with your hair set.

For easy-pack rollers, use balloons that are slightly inflated. Anchor the hair with special hair tape that will not pull. Don't try to sleep in the balloons—but you'll probably not have to; hair dries quickly using this method.

You can set your hair and arrange it at the same time. Brush hair to top of head and pin with a large barrette (never a rubber band—it tears hair). Twist the remaining ends and anchor under the knot. Your hair will be softly curled when you let it down.

Oily hair can cause pimples and blackheads at the edges of your hairline. Clean your hairline carefully. You can wash your hair every day; wet hair doesn't cause colds.

Use bone, shell, or ivory combs for your hair. They tend to be gentle on the hair. (They make a super gift to a special friend.)

Setting hair with diet gelatin—grape for dark hair, lemon for blondes—gives it color and bounce. And because it's dietetic, the gelatin contains no sugar granules.

Skin

A mixture of potter's clay (kaolin) and water makes a fast effective masque for oily skin.

Skin should be exfoliated by brushing and washing. The older you are, the greater the need for ridding your skin surface of these dead cells.

Keep several bottles around filled with spring or distilled water for your face.

Avoid deodorant soaps if you work outdoors, especially in the sun. Some of the ingredients may form a chemical reaction that will stain your skin.

A quick and easy exercise to firm a jawline is trying to touch your nose with the end of your tongue.

Open your eyes as if you are surprised for an easy lid-firming exercise that can be done behind dark sunglasses.

The old formula of a cup of hot water and lemon juice every morning still works.

Dramatic changes in the skin temperature can break delicate capillaries and cause spidery lines. Avoid going outside and inside too often.

Drink bottled water when traveling; it is better for your digestive system and for your skin, too.

Sesame oil or vegetable shortening makes an excellent skin lubricant or cleanser.

Rub the soles of your feet and elbows with toothpaste or powder; it will smooth rough skin.

Use an old toothbrush to massage the soles of your feet if you have a tendency to get calluses.

Makeup

Charcoal color above the eyes is universally flattering; it should be gently applied from an ordinary soft pencil and thinned to a soft gray.

Use a foundation that is a shade or two lighter than your usual foundation in a wrinkled area.

Wear makeup that includes skin-protecting ingredients; always wear it if you live in a polluted area. Makeup is often better for your skin than the smog or particles in the air.

The old "Southern belle" trick of lightly pinching your cheeks instead of using rouge is still good; and the pinching encourages blood circulation.

Petroleum jelly can be used on the lips and eyebrows.

Add fullness to your lips with a slightly lighter shade in the center.

Open your eye and intensify the color by lining the inside of the lid with blue for brown eyes and violet for blue or green eyes.

Mix brown and beige lipstick with your red lipstick and dab a bit of gloss over it all for a super-sparkle evening look.

Don't forget to color the tops and lobes of ears with blusher or better, cream blusher.

Be sure to apply foundation to the edges of your jaw—and under your earlobes. Line the collar of your sweater or blouse with toweling before applying foundation to avoid staining your clothes.

Dab a bit of color on your arms when you wear a short-sleeved blouse in the summer; you'll look rosy and smooth.

A light brushing of powder in a bronze tone used by many black women can make a white woman look healthy and glowing.

Try new makeups around the house; you should feel comfortable in a new effect—just as you should in a new outfit.

You can make your own lip template from a sheet of stiff plastic. Just place over your lips and color in—sure shape, every time.

Don't forget your eyelids when applying foundation.

Castor oil makes your lashes lustrous.

Dusting your lashes with cornstarch makes the mascara adhere; the powder can also be used between coats.

Use eyeshadow for face sculpturing. Use the white and frosted shades on the sides of the face to produce quick rounding for a haggard visage.

Poorly plucked brows are worse than naturally unruly ones — no matter how bad they are. If you can't pluck correctly, trim with a small nail scissors, and groom with petroleum jelly.

You can make a quick makeup by mixing powder with a tiny bit of moisturizer.

Thin a creamy makeup with water. The oils in the makeup will hold the water in suspension and keep it fresh longer. Use the palm of your hand as a palette.

Be sure your lashes are dry before applying mascara. They must be moisture- and oil-free to hold mascara.

SPECIAL APPROACHES TO WORKING BEAUTY

Whether you work indoors or outdoors, you may be suffering from dehydrated skin, skin that ages early and looks dull and drab. For prevention and elimination of wrinkles, sags, age spots, and cellulite the following are recommended:

- Willpower, management of stress
- A good cleansing and nourishing program for the skin
- Exercise of the whole body — including the neck and face
- A good diet that includes at least 8 glasses of water a day. (The diet should include beauty foods to put *on* your face as well as *in* your stomach.)

This four-path approach will keep you lovely all your life long.

Many working women should consider the "special" help of a special beauty week. If you have two weeks of paid vacation, it can be more helpful and restful to spend one of those weeks completely devoted to a dramatic change.

Stain and Spot Removal

Accidents happen. There is little as irritating as a spot or stain on one of your carefully selected office outfits. And there is little that can damage a well-groomed appearance as easily or completely as a stain. A perfectly made-up face will lose some of its allure if gum is stuck to your skirt or grease is on your blouse.

Treat a stain as promptly as possible. It is best to do something before the stain-making substance dries. Fresh stains are easier to remove than old set ones.

Before using any remover on colored clothes, experiment with a section in a seam or some other inconspicuous part of the garment.

If you don't know what substance caused the stain, wash the stain lightly with cold water. Sponge with the water and allow to dry. If the stain is still evident, try cleaning fluid.

The first step in stain removal is identifying the source. Here is how that is done:

Color: Sometimes you can identify the source just from looking at the mark; ink tends to penetrate, oil tends to follow the weave of the fabric, and paint or a liquid paper or white-out tends to build up on the surface.

Smell: The odor can be used to identify food, medicinal, or perfume stains.

Location: Obviously, a stain under the arm of a silk blouse is more likely to come from perspiration than from food; and a stain on your skirt front might have come from lunch.

Touch: The texture of the offensive mark might help to identify it; glue is sticky, fingernail polish and white-out build up.

After you know the origin of the stain, you can decide the best way of removing it. Here is a short list:

Remove with Dry Solvent	Remove with Water
carbon	eggs
carbon paper	animal glues (mailing packages,
ballpoint pen	etc., often use this type)
gum	blood
nail polish	cream
oils	leather dyes
paints	writing inks and art materials
plastic adhesives	liquor
	soft drinks
	beer
	tea
	tobacco

Floating the stain away: This is a very important method of removal, and it is especially good in removing insoluble substances. Soak the stain in water or other liquid.

Absorbing the substance: This is good for nubby or piled fabrics. Sprinkle the powder over the stain; the stain substance is then absorbed into the particles.

Chemical action: This is the basis for many commercial chemical spot remover formulas. The idea is that the remover and the substance that has stained the garment combine and form a totally new substance, and the new substance just washes away.

Mechanical action: This means brushing, rubbing, or chipping the stain or spot away.

Enzyme action: Special chemicals actually digest the material that created the stain.

When removing a stain, you should take some simple measures as described below.

- Stained fabrics should not be pressed.
- Wash the stain as soon as possible. Blot and soak it between two towels in the ladies' room.
- Fabric has a tendency to ring; brush lightly and rapidly from the center of the stained area to the outer edge. Continue one or two inches beyond the stain.
- Store cleaning supplies in a cool dark place. A bottom drawer is perfect. Be sure that you keep the directions and that bottles are well-marked so no one can mistake them for beverages.

   Below is a list of cleaning equipment you should keep in your desk and a small chart that you might want to keep with the cleaning equipment.

   In plastic bags, keep absorbents such as corn meal, cornstarch, or fuller's earth. In small cosmetic bottles, keep bleach, peroxide, white vinegar, acetone, alcohol. In a small box or plastic container, keep cotton, towels, tissue, a small toothbrush, sponges, a medicine dropper, and a bit of soap.

Stain and Spot Removal Chart

Stain	Washable Fabrics	Other Fabrics
Beverages (alcoholic and soft drinks)	Soak in cold water, wash in warm suds, rinse well. Soak silk, wool, or colored items for half hour in 2 tablespoons hydrogen peroxide to 1 gallon water. Soak white linen, rayon, and cotton 15 minutes in 1 tablespoon household bleach to 1 quart water	Dry clean
Blood	Soak in lukewarm water. Wash in enzyme-containing detergent product	Treat with cold water to which table salt has been added. Rinse well, blot with towel
Chewing gum	Scrape gum from surface with dull knife. Soak spot in cleaning fluid	Scrape gum away
Chocolate or coffee	Soak in warm water	Sponge with dry-cleaning agent
Deodorants (cream, stick or spray variety)	Wash in detergent and hot water	Sponge with dry-cleaning agent
Grass	Wash in detergent	Dry clean
Grease and tar	Place towel under stain. Dab cleaning fluid on area	Dry clean

Stain	Washable Fabrics	Other Fabrics
Ink	Pour water through stained area; repeat until bleeding stops. If stain doesn't bleed, wash in detergent and white vinegar. Some rust removers can be used alone or in combination with above treatment. Also try household ammonia	Dry clean
Ink, ballpoint pen, felt-tipped pen	Place blotter under fabric; drip cleaning fluid through spot; soak in solution of detergent and warm water	Dry clean
Lipstick	Turn garment inside out; place stain over absorbent towel; pour cleaning fluid through stain; blot dry	Same as washable fabric
Makeup	Pretreat with detergent; launder	Dab with cleaning fluid
Milk, cream, ice cream, coffee with cream	Soak in warm water	Sponge with cleaning fluid
Paint	Sponge with paint thinner as soon as possible	Dry clean
Perspiration	Launder in soapy hot water	Sponge with water
Perfume or cologne	Wash immediately in detergent and hot water; don't let stain dry	Dry clean
Shoe polish	Sponge with alcohol; wash in hot water	Dry clean
Tea	Launder	Sponge with water
Water spots	Launder	Wipe with damp cloth

Favorable Outlook for Women's Employment

The best paying and most prestigious jobs are those in the professional and technical areas. The percentage of women in such careers has increased in the last twenty years, and many of these areas would provide excellent opportunities for reentry women as well as for young women starting out. Right now women make up:

- 63 percent of all social workers;
- 69 percent of teachers in elementary schools;
- 70 percent of health and dental technicians;
- 82 percent of librarians;
- 93 percent of dietitians; and
- 97 percent of registered nurses.

But, women are under-represented in male-dominated professions such as law, medicine, architecture, and engineering.

During the 1970s, women started entering training for nontraditional professions. Of the ten runners-up for the 1980 Miss America Contest, four were enrolled in law school or planned to be lawyers. In a recent survey conducted by the

177

American Council on Education, 17 percent of women college freshmen intended to become business executives, doctors, lawyers, or engineers. A similar study conducted only twenty years ago showed only 6 percent of women were interested in entering these fields.

Here is a list of professional occupations that seem to be attracting women. One of the reasons that they do attract women is that trained people can find jobs in these fields, and there seems to be less divergence in the salary paid.

Law. The mind knows no sex. Women have proven to be excellent lawyers with a true sense of justice and the bravery to confront difficult situations. Twenty-four percent of all law students are now women.

Pharmacy. The complexities of formulas and the job of dealing with the public can be turned into a good position in pharmacies. Thirty-seven percent of all pharmacists are women.

Medicine. The proportion of first-year medical students rose from 8 percent in 1965 to 22 percent just ten years later.

Veterinary medicine. Women have more than doubled their percentage of enrollment between 1970 and 1980. The increase in small animals as pets and the interest in animals and their health make this a growing field. With women jockeys come horse-trainers and veterinarians.

Architecture. Innovative, practical ideas on providing for our population means additional opportunities. The woman who could only aspire to be a decorator can now plan the building she wants to decorate. Twelve percent of all architects are women.

Dentistry. Here is a good bet that women are missing. Many women are technicians, but the enrollment for women in dental colleges rose only 7 percent in the past fifteen years. Dexterity, calm, and care are needed—abilities that have always been assigned to women.

Engineering. Fewer than 1 percent of the engineers were women in the late sixties; now, about 6 percent are women. This is an area of increased importance, and there will be great varieties of employment possibilities for engineers in the next ten years.

Optometry. From 3 percent in the sixties to 11 percent now. But, the potential for convenient work, good working hours, and creative work possibilities is excellent. The overall picture is encouraging. The past decade's progress in professional jobs means that this area is ready for women.

The chart below gives a more complete prediction of the possible openings within the next few years.

	Total employment 1974	Average annual openings 1974-85
PROFESSIONAL		
Accountant	805,000	45,500
Chemist	135,000	6,400
Computer programmer	200,000	13,000
Dentist	105,000	6,200
Economist	71,000	4,700
Engineers	1,100,000*	
Civil	170,000	9,300
Electrical	290,000	12,200
Industrial	180,000	7,200
Mechanical	185,000	7,900
Petroleum/Mining	17,000	1,100
Geologist	23,000	1,300
Optometrist	19,000	900
Physician	350,000	23,000
Physicist	48,000	1,700
Systems analyst	115,000	9,100
Veterinarian	29,000	1,450
TECHNICAL		
Drafter	313,000	17,300
Engineering and science technician	560,000	32,000
MANAGERS AND ADMINISTRATORS		
Bank officer	240,000	16,000
City manager	2,900	150
Hospital/health administrator	150,000	17,400
Purchasing agent	189,000	11,700
SALES WORKERS		
Insurance agent, broker, underwriter	470,000	19,400
Manufacturers' salesworker	380,000	9,500
Wholesale trade salesworker	770,000	30,000
Securities salesworker	100,000	6,100
CRAFT WORKERS		
Air conditioning, refrigeration, and heating mechanic	200,000	10,900
Aircraft mechanic	130,000	3,200
Automobile mechanic	735,000	24,400
Business machine repairer	65,000	3,100

	Total employment 1974	Average annual openings 1974-85
Carpenter	1,060,000	49,100
Computer service technician	50,000	4,300
Electrician		
Construction	245,000	11,700
Maintenance	280,000	13,800
Industrial machinery repairer	500,000	42,500
Painter	450,000	16,700
Plumber and pipefitter	375,000	23,500
Television and radio service technician	135,000	6,600
Welder	645,000	27,000

How to Write a Resume

Books have been written on how to write and use a resume, but this book is about beauty, and the job of the resume is only to get you an interview for the job you want.

If the resume can get you an interview, it has accomplished its task. The best resumes—the most effective ones—are short, seldom more than one page in length. They are also selective. One resume is seldom enough to describe anyone for every job. Your home office should include three or four rough drafts of resumes that can be edited to fit job descriptions as they appear in newspapers or in employment offices.

The first step in a successful job interview is getting the interview. A resume, or a letter requesting the interview, is the standard way to introduce yourself. People are forever telling stories about resumes on red paper, pop-ups, or other attention-getting devices. I think they probably get attention; but they probably don't get the interview, or the job.

Some resume writers include long-range and short-range career objectives, and some even include a listing of personal strengths.

There is some optional data that can be included, depending on the situation, the type of job, and even used as a way of alerting a prospective employer of possible special problems:

- Age, or date of birth (no employer should ask this)
- Marital or personal living arrangements
- Children or dependants
- Place of birth or citizenship

- Ability to travel easily or willingness to relocate
- General health
- Hobbies and special interests
- Religion (only if special diet or unusual schedule is needed)
- Political interests (only if very active or later revelation might be embarrassing)

It is usually unwise to provide too lengthy a list of your needs, abilities, desires, and personality. It almost announces that you are unflexible, and that dealing with you will be on your own terms—only. Besides, no one sees us as we see ourselves, and it might be fun to have someone open another door to our own self-concept.

Uppermost in any resume should be clarity, ease in reading, and direct well-organized information. After you have carefully typed your resume, mail a copy to yourself. When you receive it, you'll be amazed to see how it affects you from a different perspective.

One of the best ways of starting the resume is to honestly describe yourself. If you had to describe yourself in three phrases, what would they be?

- A wife, a mother, a woman?
- A secretary, an organizer, a bowler?
- A gourmet, a painter, a technician?

If you have done this spontaneously, you've probably listed the priorities in your own value system. It is good to follow them. If you see yourself first as a wife and mother, you'll have to consider how the job will affect that part of your life. If you really are interested in fine foods, you should make sure that the job you go after will provide enough time for the exploration and experimentation that a true wine-food lover needs.

The most important element in any job is the actual work and the actual pay for that work. The products you are selling at the job interview are your time and your knowledge. Although key employees are an important asset for any company, an applicant is usually hired to perform a specific task or provide a skill that is needed at the time of the job opening. Personnel are just too expensive to hire for some "perhaps" future need. So, you should remember that you are being hired not for potential, but for work.

You will not be happy in a job that you don't really like, so you won't look well in that job. You must actually enjoy the activity of the work, and be proud to be associated with your craft.

The Two Week On-the-Job Beauty Program

The time is now! Start the program now, if it is a weekday. The program starts on a Monday and goes through ten workdays, or two work weeks. It has been divided by days, and by seven basic beauty areas: hand care, hair care, skin care, makeup, exercise, diets, and a special tip for special problems.

After the day-by-day directions is a special chart. The chart is only to keep your own record. It is simply a way of reminding yourself to do something for beauty. Beauty, like what you eat, how you talk, and the hundreds of other small familiar activities each day, is usually a matter of habit. The program and the chart are designed to break old habits and form new habits. "Looking great" can be *your* habit.

Monday (first day)

Hand Care: Massage hand cream into your fingers, the backs of your hands, and your wrists. Keep hand cream, emery boards, scissors, nail brush, cuticle cream, orangewood sticks in your desk drawer or handbag kit.

Hair care: Starting today, brush your hair for a few minutes every day. Always be gentle; if you get stuck on a tangle, hold your hair and gently work the snarl

	out—never force or tear at the hair. Keep a small natural brush, a rubber or plastic comb in your desk or handbag.
Skin care:	Wash your face. Rinse with cool or tepid water until your face is absolutely clean. Examine your skin and decide if it is normal, dry, or oily. Keep moisturizer, foundation, and clean cotton balls in your desk or bag.
Makeup:	Examine the edges of your makeup—your hairline and your jawline. Is the shade you are wearing really right? There should be no line or color change between your face and neck. If you need new makeup, buy it now.
Exercise/ Fitness:	There must be a door someplace in your office; open it. Stand, with your feet on the floor, toes pointed ahead, and hold the doorknobs; one in each hand. Take a step to the right, keeping your buttocks tucked under, bend the right leg, at the knee. Keep the left leg straight, and flat on the floor. Repeat with alternate legs. That exercise should limber you and make you graceful. Do it when unobserved.
Diet:	Start your own diet chart. Use 10 small pieces of paper or index cards. Write the day and date on each. Keep the card in your desk, locker, or purse. Write *everything* you eat and drink on the cards.
Special problems:	You know what yours are. Look in the index and find the beauty area. Read as much as you can before you plan your own personal program.

Tuesday (second day)

Hand care:	Wash hands and apply hand cream. To rid your fingertips of dry or overgrown cuticles use a cuticle remover cream. Apply it carefully over the cuticles and after a moment or two push back the cuticle with your orangewood stick.
Hair care:	For the minimum hair care short hair is best. But you'll have to sacrifice versatility. Unless you can wear your hair in at least two different ways you'll probably grow tired of the style. Experiment with a new style that might work well for your hair-and lifestyle.

Skin care: Discourage skin blemishes by keeping skin clean and pores unclogged through scrubbing away dead skin cells. An extra two glasses of water each day will also insure clearer, blemish-free skin.

Makeup: Using your makeup kit and your usual makeup, experiment with the effects you can get by changing the intensity and depth of the color at various spots. Buy a set of small sable paint brushes, available at any art store. They are easy to control, and wash and dry easily.

Exercise/
Fitness: A feeling of lethargy is usually a sign of boredom. Some tasks at work are unpleasant and unexciting. Do the unpleasant or boring task as quickly as possible and then reward yourself with some simple exercises: Spread your arms; make a fist, rotate slowly 5 times. Stretch your legs, rotate your feet at the ankles 5 times. Breathe deeply 5 times.

Diet: Confine snacks to carrot sticks brought from home. Most coffee shops serve about 3 oz. of meat in a sandwich. Get used to measuring—by eye—the food that you eat.

Special
problems: People who are prone to ingrown hair should be very cautious about waxing excessive hair; use tweezers instead.

Wednesday (third day)

Hand care: Nails grow about one-quarter of an inch a month. It will take six months to grow the length of the nail. Massage the area close to your first knuckle, it sometimes stimulates growth.

Hair care: If your hair texture is wispy and fly-away, you can set your hair with tape. When your hair is almost dry, use a piece of hairset tape about a yard long, to anchor it smoothly. The air will dry your hair in a bunch and it will seem less fly-away.

Skin care: Be consistent; to see results you have to be patient for at least three weeks. Never wash your face directly before going out on a cold day; cold is very drying, and you will risk chapped skin around the eyes and mouth. Always wear a scarf in the winter to protect the delicate skin on the neck.

Makeup: Dark circles under your eyes can be hidden with thin light cream. Blend moisturizer with the cover stick, being careful to match the color with your skin. Circles can be caused by air pollution.

Exercise/ Fitness: Sitting at your desk chair, hold the edge of the desk firmly and push against it. Then pull up, trying to lift it (you'll not be able to). This exercise firms your chest and the muscles under your breast.

Diet: Biting and eating can really be an expression of anger. Every time you find yourself biting, stop and think: Am I really angry, bored, worried, tired, or feeling sorry for myself? Count to ten, and try to identify your emotion.

Special problems: Moles and birthmarks can be removed through modern technology. Laser beams are now being used to banish wine-marks. Write to your local or state medical association.

Thursday (fourth day)

Hand care: If you are under forty and have ridges on your nails, check your diet. To rid yourself of the ridges, file lightly across the surface of the nail and then buff in the same direction with a puffing powder and a soft leather or chamois cloth. Buffing stimulates the circulation in the nail bed.

Hair care: Too much hair in the wrong places can be as much or more of a problem than any other. Cold cream, or other moisturizer, does not stimulate hair growth. Most hair on the face can be concealed by bleaching. Take care of it today.

Skin care: Air conditioning in offices and large buildings often reduces humidity. If superficial lines and rough texture seem to increase during the day, freshen your face with sprays of water, in the same way you would mist a plant. A light spray will not affect your makeup.

Makeup: Match your eye makeup colors with the outfit you are wearing: wines and crimsons with soft gray and smoky blues; oranges and earth shades with browns, mossy greens, and corals; beiges and whites with golden brown, russets, and peach colors.

Exercise/ Fitness: Sitting at your desk or work place, hold onto the edges of your chair. Tighten your body as you push down with your arms and attempt to lift yourself from your chair. Repeat 3 times. Do Wednesday's chest exercises 3 times, and then repeat the waistline-tightening exercise above.

Diet: If you brown-bag it, include vegetables, fruit, and a piece of medium-hard cheese or a hard-cooked egg. The harder the cheese, the higher in calories.

Special problems: After pregnancy or the rapid loss of weight, stretch marks can appear. Recently plastic surgery has been used to remove these marks; best of all is avoiding them altogether. Keep your thighs, hips, and body covered with moisturizer. Happily, the marks fade very slightly with time.

Friday (fifth day)

Hand care: A good patch kit will mend splits and breaks in a few minutes. When working with your hands, remember, healing may be slow.

Hair care: Cutting hair will not make it grow faster but regular trims do make the hair look better. Hair seems to grow fastest between the ages of fifteen and about twenty-five, so the woman just starting on her career should be prepared to get a trim every few months.

Skin care: Place a small tray of water near your office heater or air conditioner. You might want to keep a small fishtank on your desk instead of a plant. The water can be replaced every morning, and your skin and hair as well as your breathing will benefit from the additional moisture.

Makeup: Take all your makeup from your desk or kit, wash all brushes, and refill bottles or small vials. Learn one new idea in makeup application each day of your program.

Exercise/ Fitness: While sitting, keep your arms straight and hands on the chair. Press your buttocks together, and push down with your arms. Hold a few seconds and repeat 5 times. Repeat the chest-breast exercise from Wednesday and the waistline exercise of Thursday several times; then repeat this buttock and hip exercise.

Diet: Make lunch today your big meal of the day. For your evening meal, select a clear soup, some light protein—such as an egg or a few shrimp—and a small piece of fruit for dessert. Stave off hunger with a glass of tomato juice.

Special problems: Scars on the face, hands, or body are embarrassing. Large acne cysts can be treated with cortisone. Some raised scars can be made less noticeable after a series of steroid injections. Probably your scars will go unnoticed at work; avoid calling attention to them by dramatizing another area of your face.

Monday (sixth day)

Hand care: Yellow nails can come from continually wearing polish, smoking, or medication. The little white spots come from air pockets that are formed as the nail grows. They are harmless, but gentle treatment of your fingertips will help to reduce them. Keep a pair of thin rubber gloves in your desk if you often handle chemicals (white-out, glues, and rubber cement are chemicals).

Hair care: Air conditioning, heating, cold weather, changes in moisture and barometric pressure all affect your hair. Strive for a frame to your face that will be comfortable, soft, clean, and shining.

Skin care: Most people have combination skin. If you do, keep both types of makeup in your makeup case. Be sure you always apply moisturizer to your eyes, neck, and the backs of your hands, even if enlarged pores and an occasional break-out tell you your skin is oily. Pat the moisturizer in without dragging the skin.

Makeup: Try for a see-through glaze rather than opaque coverage. Apply two or three very thin light coats of foundation and then blush or color. After all your makeup is applied, check your blusher again; be sure it doesn't overpower or vanish in comparison to your lip color.

Exercise/ Fitness: While seated, place your hands on the back of the seat part of the chair. Lean back and straighten legs, pushing hard and lifting your entire body from the chair while tensing your thighs and hips. Repeat the chest-breast, waistline, and buttocks exercises, and then this hip-firmer again.

Diet: Memorize the following calorie counts:

- a tablespoon of margarine   100
- a slice of bread   70
- 1/4 pint ice cream   140
- French dressing   65

Are these little extras really worth it?

Special problems: Psoriasis affects a large number of people. Ask a dermatologist about the new "black light" treatment. Exposure to the sun is often helpful. This is one time that the usual warning against sun should be ignored.

Tuesday (seventh day)

Hand care: Don't use your nails as tools. Keep a small screwdriver and a pair of pliers in your desk if you frequently open bottles and jars.

Hair care: The following lengths and facial combinations work best for easy all-day care:

- Fine hair and a round face—chin length
- Straight hair and a round face—shoulder length
- Coarse hair and a pointed chin—collar length
- Thick hair and an oval face—any length
- Curly hair and a broad face—ear length
- Curly hair and a narrow face—shoulder length

Skin care: Most mud and grainy masques are for oily skin, but even a dry skin can benefit from a once-a-week stimulating treatment. Masques help to rid your skin of dead cells. Most skin cells die and flake away every four or five hours. That means that if you leave for work at 8 A.M., by noon there are dead cells on your face.

Makeup: Buy a new shade of lipstick; something that is quite different for you. Does anyone notice?

Exercise/ Fitness: This is another exercise to be done with your chair. Sit with your arms relaxed. Straighten one leg and raise it slightly, just so it clears the floor; count to 3. Straighten the other leg, and raise; flex and straighten and raise alternate legs. Repeat other desk exercises. This exercise will strengthen the back of the thighs, and will also firm the torso.

Diet: Here are some extra-easy ideas that you can enjoy on the job: a piece of fruit (except grapes and cherries), stick foods, the usual carrots and celery or asparagus and sticks of raw zucchini; also include slices of melon when they are in season.

Special problems: Uneven skin pigmentation is never attractive and spots on the hands are a sign of aging. You cannot prevent freckles and marks completely, but they can be minimized with creams containing hydroclinique. These creams often help clear other conditions, such as acne, as well.

Wednesday (eighth day)

Hand care: Avoid sun, cold, chlorine or salt water; they dry the nails and make them brittle. Don't cut nails with clippers, and use scissors as seldom as possible. Cutting and clipping encourages breaks and splits. Keep your nails filed.

Hair care: Today is the day to clean your brush and comb. Wash in tepid water and light soap. Loosen the clogged hairs from the bristles with an old comb or small brush. Shake the excess moisture from the brush and comb and allow to dry naturally, away from any heat source.

Skin care: Pantyhose can cause irritations; the lack of air circulation can create a moist environment where organisms grow. If you worry about odors, discharges, or itching, buy only hose with cotton panty inserts.

Makeup: Your brows are easily forgotten, but a very important element in your face. Make sure that they are the right arch and length to balance.

Exercise/ Fitness: When standing on the elevator, waiting, filing, or just standing on line, firm calf muscles by lifting heels as high as possible off the floor. Hold for a few seconds; repeat 3 times.

Diet: Does everyone need three meals a day? Probably not.

Many people feel better just snacking every few hours. Others find eating one meal a day can help them stay on their diet. Drink at least 8 glasses of water each day of your diet. Water will make you feel better, and avoid excessive breath and body odor that bother dieters.

Special problems: If your skin feels taut and dry after washing, you are using the wrong kind of skin cleanser. Look for mild super-fatted soap for dry skin, if you are bothered by a mask-like pulling sensation. If your skin feels greasy after washing, look for a low-alkaline soap. If you can, use your own soap rather than depending on the cleansers available in most washrooms.

Thursday (ninth day)

Hand care: Hangnails—the splits in the skin along the side of the nails—result from dryness. They can also develop from picking the skin around the nail when you are nervous. Paper cuts can also cause these small painful fissures. Keep hand lotion nearby, and rub it into your fingertips every chance you get. Smooth hands get fewer paper cuts.

Hair care: Before changing your hair color, consider the time and effort for upkeep. You can get a lasting noticeable change only with a permanent hair color product that is hard on the hair. If you change your hair color, change your entire makeup palette.

Skin care: If you smoke, or use perfume, you may develop yellow stains on your fingertips. Scrub the stained fingers with a brush to remove some of the outer dead cells, then use vinegar or lemon juice to bleach the stain. A yellow stain from perfume on the back of your ear, or from deodorant on your armpit, can be treated the same way.

Makeup: Dark complexions need cheek color to define cheek bones and accent skin tones. Look for clear, vivid hues.
Most important is a foundation shade that will even skin tone. Use two or more shades on various parts of the face for an even all-over tone.

Exercise/
Fitness:
Stand in a relaxed position, feet together. Twist your body so that your left shoulder is as far to the right as possible; and then reverse and move the right shoulder as far to the left as possible. Repeat the calf muscle exercises and this waist-trimming exercise.

Diet:
Your best choice for restaurant food is steamed, broiled, or baked dishes. Reject fried and simmered foods. Eat only half of what is on your plate. Use your will power and don't "clean your plate"; you are no longer a "good little girl."

Special
problems:
Your hair shape should take your total body shape into consideration. For limp stringy hair, towel dry to add body; if your hair falls in clumps and separates, change your haircut; if your hair will not hold a set, you should consider a body wave; if your hair is dull, make your final shampoo rinse very cool water, avoid blow dryers for at least a month.

Friday (tenth and last day)

Hand care:
Cracked skin around the fingers and nails can be a sign of allergies. Many people are allergic to common metals and if you use scissors, or metal tools, during your work, you may develop tiny bumps or dermatitis. Your hands reveal your general health in a single glance or gesture.

Hair care:
Don't ignore your hairstyle when buying sweaters and blouses; they all have to work together to make your face look its loveliest. Wear a hairstyle that shows your ears if possible. (The more of your ears you show, the more people will trust you. It is odd, but this idea probably comes from the fact that you are showing that you hear what they are saying.)

Skin care:
Don't peer at yourself in a magnifying mirror. No one, not even a new baby, has perfect skin. Other people will not notice most blemishes. Forget yourself; the paradox is that the less you worry, the better you will actually look. Worry is the enemy of beauty.

Makeup:
Heavy, dark, or uneven brows can be bleached to better balance your face. If your eyes are the focal point of your face, keep the brows well brushed and lightly covered with gloss. Clear lip gloss will help to train unruly brows.

Exercise/ Fitness:
Go through your desk-exercise program as fast as possible; then standing, repeat all these exercises. Do you feel better? Results will be slow, but soon you'll feel energetic flexibility.

Diet:
Think thin and healthy: Every time you see a tempting goodie, think about how wonderful you'll look five pounds thinner. You are strong and brave—you can conquer pastry, chocolates, or any other villains.

Special problems:
Make a list of all the good things about you. Study these things you like about yourself, and make sure you appreciate yourself. You'll be surprised at how problems fade when you don't agonize.

Take the time to do something for yourself each day, in each area, for two weeks. Allow at least thirty minutes each day for yourself. That will be five hours for the two-week program. It will serve as a good start in your total beauty program.

	Mon.	Tue.	Wed.	Thurs.	Fri.	Mon.	Tue.	Wed.	Thurs.	Fri.
Hand care:										
Hair care:										
Skin care:										
Makeup:										
Exercise/ Fitness:										
Diet:										
Special Problems:										

The next group of suggestions are not for nine-to-five; they are for at-home care. Keeping yourself groomed at home will make your daily office-job beauty care easier and more effective.

Mornings:

1. Stretch arms and legs while still in bed.
2. Breathe deeply and slowly for at least a minute.
3. Drink water, juice, or beverage.
4. Wake-up exercises.
5. Cleanse, tone, and moisturize face and neck; apply body lotion to legs in winter, arms in summer.
6. Apply makeup, arrange hair, dress for work.

Evenings:

1. Relax, exercise, or just stretch to ease work muscles.
2. Cleanse face, neck, and body.
3. Bath (unless preferred in morning).
4. Hair massage, scalp brushing, and hair setting.
5. Body lotion in cold and dry climates.
6. Teeth and gum care, flossing.
7. Facial or special exercises.

Special Bi-weekly:

(Thursday and Sunday nights seem to be most women's favorite evenings for grooming.)

1. Shampoo and rinse.
2. Masque for oily skin, or exfoliation for very oily skin.

Weekly:

1. Manicure and pedicure.
2. Special wash and, after examination of hair ends, conditioning if needed.
3. Masque for oily or dry skin.
4. Shave or depilatorize legs and underarms.
5. Examine clothes for raveled hems, loose buttons, spots, etc.
6. Clean shoes, check heels.
7. Check handbag, clean and refresh makeup kit, etc.

Epilogue

Career women, from executives to models, from telephone-repair persons to actresses, and even public representatives are all aware of beauty. The most important element in looking good is feeling good about yourself.

During the past decade, there has been great emphasis on women joining the business ranks and becoming equal to men in every way—as part of that equality, women are responsible to be the kind of people that we admire most. Many of the books and magazines that you've read are guidebooks for those who want to be female hoodlums—mugging with words and stealing credit for work. Beauty is as beauty does; be for yourself first, but make sure that there is something left over for others. You'll be happier for it.

When you decide to be beautiful on the job, you are not exercising vanity, you are evidencing a zest for life and a sense of responsibility, not for yourself alone but for all those you care about, meaning, of course—if you choose—everyone.

You must make a certain commitment of time. But more, you must make a commitment of thought. Your decision to be beautiful at work means that you will begin, if you have not done so already, to do all of the following:

- To control your diet by choosing foods that are better for your health and vitality because that's what your beauty is dependent on.
- To control your thoughts, since negative thinking and the stress and scowls that tension breeds cause poor posture, sagging muscles, and skin problems.
- To plan your wardrobe to choose colors and fabrics, styles, and fashions that best project your own unique style, your own special beauty.

196

- To choose your friends and associates—to eliminate those who impose too great a drain on your energies, spirit, time, and thought when there is no return contribution.
- To develop the empathy to see the good in your co-workers so that you can go forward to success without guilt, office politics, or unpleasantness.
- To develop your job and the tasks that are assigned to you to find creative outlets, stimulate your mind, and provide you with challenges and satisfactions.
- To develop patience to work until you achieve your goals.
- To develop faith and hope to free you from fear of the future, and above all, to develop the will to surround yourself with an atmosphere of beauty, happiness, and love. Love is the best work-time beautifier of all—and that means giving love to every activity even more than being loved, and having status.

Bibliography

Alberti, Robert, Ph.D., and Emmons, Michael, *Stand Up, Speak Out, Talk Back: The Key to Self-Assertive Behavior.* New York: 1977. 206 pp.

Barrett, Rona. *How You Can Look Rich and Achieve Sexual Ecstasy.* New York: Bantam Books, 1978.

Bartusis, Mary Ann, M.D. *Every Other Man.* New York: E. P. Dutton, 1978.

Benson, Herbert. *The Mind/Body Effect: How Behavioral Medicine Can Show You the Way to Better Health.* New York: Simon & Schuster, 1979. 190 pp.

Blanda, George, and Herskowitz, Micky. *Over Forty: Feeling Great, and Looking Good!* New York: Simon & Schuster, 1978.

Broderick, Dr. Carlfred. *Couples: How to Confront Problems and Maintain Loving Relationships.* New York: Simon & Schuster, 1979. 224 pp.

Carnes, Ralph and Valerie. *Body Sculpture: Weight Training for Women.* New York: Simon & Schuster, 1978. 192 pp.

Employment and Earnings, October 1978, U.S. Department of Labor, Bureau of Labor Statistics, Vol. 25, No. 10.

Employment in Perspective: Working Women. Report 544, No. 2, Second Quarter, 1978.

Fast, Julius. *Body Language.* New York: Pocketbooks, 1977. 181 pp.

Friday, Nancy. *My Mother, My Self: A Daughter's Search for Identity.* New York: Dell Publishing Company, 1977. 475 pp.

Grossman, Richard. *Choosing & Changing: A Guide to Self-Reliance.* New York: E. P. Dutton, 1978. 132 pp.

Harragan, Betty Lehan. *Games Mother Never Taught You.* New York: Warner Books, 1977. 399 pp.

Hening, Margaret, and Jardim, Anne. *The Managerial Woman.* New York: Pocketbooks, 1977. 256 pp.

Korda, Michael. *Success!* New York: Ballantine Books, 1977. 297 pp.

———. *Power How to Get It, How to Use It.* New York: Ballantine Books, 1975. 311 pp.

Labor, Bureau of Labor Statistics, 1978.

Look at Hours Worked Under the Fair Labor Standards Act, U.S. Department of Labor, Employment Standards Administration, Wage and Hour Division. WH Publication 1199, revised, 1978.

Livingston, Lida, and Schrader, Constance. *Wrinkles: How To Prevent Them, How To Erase Them.* Englewood Cliffs, N.J.: Prentice-Hall, Inc., 1978, 160 pp.

Kory, Robert B., and Bloomfield, Harold H. *The Holistic Way to Health & Happiness: A New Approach to Complete Lifetime Wellness.* New York: Simon & Schuster, 1978. 311 pp.

Linver, Sandy. *Speak Easy; How to Talk Your Way to the Top.* New York: Simon & Schuster, 1978. 224 pp.

Millar, Dan P., and Millar, Frank. *Messages and Myths.* New York: Alfred Publishing Company, Inc., 1976. 209 pp.

Molloy, John T. *The Woman's Dress for Success Book.* New York: Warner Books, 1977. 188 pp.

———. *Dress For Success.* New York: Warner Books, 1975.

Sakol, Jeanne. *All Day/All Night—All Woman: How to Be a Success as a Woman, 24 Hours a Day.* New York: Charles of the Ritz Group Ltd., 1978. 131 pp.

Schachter, Stanley, *Emotion Obesity and Crime.* New York: Academic Press, 1971. 96 pp.

Scheflen, Albert and Alice. *Body Language and Social Order.* Englewood Cliffs, N.J.: Prentice-Hall, Inc. Spectrum Books, 1972. 206 pp.

Schrader, Constance. *Makeovers: Changing Your Image,* Englewood Cliffs, N.J.: Prentice-Hall, Inc., 1979. 96 pp.

Seaman, Barbara, and Seaman, Gideon, M.D. *Women and the Crisis in Sex Hormones.* New York: Bantam Books, 1977. 620 pp.

Simenauer, Jacqueline, and Pietropinto, Anthony, M.D. *Beyond the Male Myth.* New York: New American Library, Signet Books, 1977. 468 pp.

Taubman, Bryna, *How to Become an Assertive Woman: The Key to Self-Fulfillment.* New York: Pocketbooks, 1976. 214 pp.

Trahey, Jane. *Women & Power: Who's Got It, How to Get It.* New York: Avon Books, 1977. 262 pp.

U.S. News & World Report, January 15, 1979, Special, "Working Women—Joys and Sorrows." Copyright 1979.

U.S. Working Women: A Data Book. U.S. Department of Labor, Bureau of Labor Statistics, 1977.

Wagenvoord, James, and Bailey, Peyton. *Men: A Book for Women.* New York: Avon Books, 1978. 369 pp.

Where to Find BLS Statistics on Women, Report 530, U.S. Department of Labor, Bureau of Labor Statistics, 1978.

Widby, Beth. *A Basic Guide to Self-Improvement for Women.* New York: Popular Library, 1977. 151 pp.

Williams, Marcille Gray, *The New Executive Woman.* Radnor, Pa.: Chilton Book Company, 1977. 233 pp.

Winston, Stephanie, *Getting Organized: The Easy Way to Put Your Life in Order.* New York: W. W. Norton & Co., 1978. 256 pp.

Index